American Law Enforcement

Vern L. Folley
Harrisburg Area Community College

American Law Enforcement

Holbrook Press, Inc.
Boston

Library of Congress Catalogue Card Number: 72-91548

Second printing . . . March, 1974

DEDICATION

to my late brother

ELWIN

who in life knew my dedication to
law enforcement, and who now, I
believe, is pleased to know this
volume is published. He yet shares
his life with me and I humbly share
this work with him.

Contents

Preface

In our modern, industrialized, urban society, law enforcement has become such an important part of life that an understanding of its development, philosophy, responsibility, and function is imperative for all citizens. A historical and philosophical perspective of law enforcement will help the citizen to better comprehend the present complicated criminal justice system, its principles, its legal authority, and its effect on society in general. Law enforcement plays a vital role in the preservation of our democratic way of life, and an understanding of this will encourage citizen support and demand for professional law enforcement services.

American Law Enforcement is designed to serve three groups of readers: 1) those who are preparing for a career in law enforcement or criminal justice, 2) those who are presently employed by a criminal justice agency who wish to increase their professional knowledge, and 3) citizens interested in an understanding of the law enforcement function and our criminal justice system.

The content of *American Law Enforcement* deals generally with broad conceptual and philosophical knowledge as well as practical implications. The fundamental concepts, the historic perspective, trends, and the primary problems faced by law enforcement agencies are presented in nontechnical language for clarity of understanding and ease of reading.

The book is divided into eight chapters, each dealing with a major area of concern or interest. Chapters 1 through 4 provide the reader an understanding of the police function, the present status of law enforcement, and its development. Subsequent chapters discuss current problems, such as crime and traffic; career opportunities; and the criminal justice process from arrest to release.

1

The Nature of
Law Enforcement

The enforcement of the law, a complicated process involving numerous agencies, is one of the most influential mechanisms for social control. In fact, there exists no governmental function that controls or directs the activities of the public as much as law enforcement. With the possible exception of education, law enforcement is the service with which the public has most frequent contact. Such contact and control is constant, and, if it is not experienced directly through personal contact, it is at least felt indirectly through the visible or implied presence of law enforcement personnel. And yet, inconsistent with its significance, law enforcement remains a subject that the public knows less about than any other governmental function. Although law enforcement is an often discussed issue, few people actually realize its significance.

Before the law enforcement student can fully understand and appreciate the full scope and nature of law enforcement, he must become familiar with certain basic components, terms, and concepts.

LAW ENFORCEMENT DEFINED

The phrase "law enforcement" correctly suggests the enforcement of the law or refers to the people who enforce the law. To most citizens the phrase "law enforcement" relates directly to a uniformed police officer or to police activities in the community. This relationship is not incorrect since the police are most surely involved in the enforcement of the law and, by definition, police officers are persons employed by a governmental agency and charged with the responsibility of enforcing the law and maintaining order. The blanket term "law enforcement officer" refers to those persons employed to enforce the law and maintain order at the several levels of government. The term "police" usually refers to law enforcement personnel at the municipal level.

Not entirely valid, however, is the tendency to think of

crime control and the maintenance of order as the exclusive responsibility of the police. This misconception is easily understood, however, when we consider the visible activities of the police. The police have the responsibility for dealing with crime on a twenty-four hour basis, are usually conspicuously visible to the public, and are the agents that immediately respond when violations of the law occur. In fact, by virtue of their continual and immediate involvement, police officers themselves often lose sight of the total system and tend to think of crime control as their exclusive domain.

This erroneous assumption of total responsibility can be detrimental to effective law enforcement and crime control. Through cooperation with other crime control agencies, law enforcement officers can insure maximum effectiveness in working toward the common objective of law enforcement. Those agencies involved in crime control and crime suppression are collectively referred to as the "criminal justice system."

CRIMINAL JUSTICE SYSTEM

The criminal justice system is the mechanism society uses to maintain the standards of conduct necessary to protect individuals and the community. This system operates by apprehending, prosecuting, convicting, and sentencing those members of society who violate legislated societal rules. It has three separately organized units consisting of *law enforcement*, *courts*, and *corrections*.

These parts are by no means independent of each other, since the activities of each has a direct effect on the others. The criminal justice system is interrelated through a smooth sequence of events usually put into motion when the police identify and arrest a violator of the law, which then necessitates court action. The court hears the case, and if a conviction results, the law violator is sentenced and referred to the proper correctional agency.

Not only is there a sequential association between units of the system, but also there are cross-directional associations. For example, the success of corrections will determine whether a convicted person will again become police business. It will also influence the courts in their sentencing. In addition, police activities and practices are subject to court scrutiny, and such activities are often determined by court decision.

Generally speaking, the police are charged with the *detection, identification,* and *apprehension* of law violators; courts *hear cases, weigh evidence, interpret law, determine guilt or innocence, sentence* the offender, and then give him *probation* or have him *incarcerated*; and corrections is charged with *detention* and *rehabilitation* of the offender. This is obviously an oversimplification of the process, but it does place in perspective the generalized role of each unit within the criminal justice system. Although criminal process is a rather orderly progression of events, it is more complicated and sophisticated than the foregoing may indicate.

In meeting their responsibilities the police become involved in complicated administrative and operational processes, such as crime prevention, patrol, investigation, and various tactical operations. In addition, police activities are always controlled and influenced by law and interpretations of law. The court process involves determination of jurisdiction, prosecution, defense, and procedural processes, such as filing the information, arraignment, trial, sentencing, appeal, etc. Corrections involves pretrial investigations, probation, parole, detention, revocation, and many treatment activities.

The criminal justice system will be given indepth coverage in subsequent chapters. The important points to recognize now are: 1) The police are but one of the three related units within the system; 2) The system includes police, courts, and corrections; 3) Each unit has different but re-

POLICE

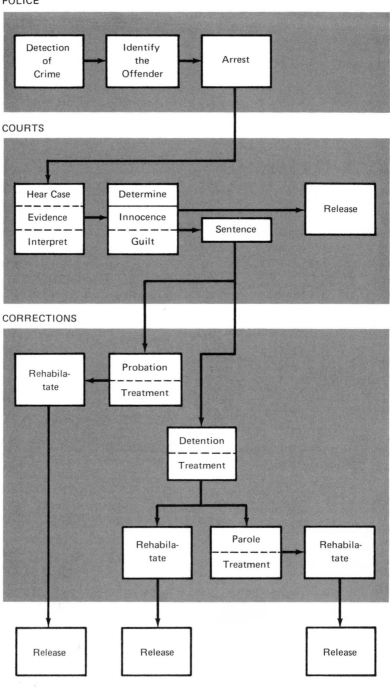

COURTS

CORRECTIONS

lated responsibilities; 4) The success of each unit influences and is influenced by the success of the others; and 5) The overall objective of all units is the control of crime and disorder.

The primary focus of this book is on the police or the law enforcement function, but this should not suggest that courts and corrections are less important. To achieve the optimum, it is obvious that efficiency in all is imperative. The police, however, hold a position of primary importance since they usually initiate action and are directly involved with the public. They are charged with performing their functions where all eyes are upon them. Most important, the police represent our first line of defense against criminality and disorder.

Since this is a time of increasing crime, increasing social unrest, and increasing public sensitivity to both, it is concurrently a time when police work is important, complicated, conspicuous, and delicate.

LAW

The foregoing discussion of law enforcement and the criminal justice system continually referred to *law*. In fact, the entire system evolved as a result of law, and its existence is controlled and directed by law. Therefore, to fully understand and appreciate law enforcement and criminal justice, we must have a full understanding of law, its definition, and its development.

Law is a blanket term for a far-reaching and complex concept that encompasses many types of law and relates to society, customs, and justice.

Black's Law Dictionary defines law simply as "that which is laid down, ordained, or established" and "that which is obeyed and followed by all citizens, subject to sanc-

7

tions or legal consequences, is a law."[1] Certainly, this over-simplifies the concept, and we must explore its development, nature, and purposes to fully appreciate it as it relates to the role of law enforcement in our modern society.

"Law" is a general term used in several contexts. For example, there is the law of contradiction which means that a proposition cannot be both true and false, the law of gravity, and the laws of the universe. Of course, the law that concerns us does not deal with scientific principles or philosophic concepts. Instead, it deals with those principles or codes of conduct considered beneficial to society.

It is significant that the use of the word "law" always relates to what is right. The French translation of law is "droit" and is defined as right. The German word for law is "recht" which also means right. We can infer that law, like morality, tells us what is right or what is wrong. In other words, law is one means of controlling conduct and is usually supported by morality. For example, the killing of another human being is a violation against morality as well as being unlawful.

Law is essential to society and forms the basis of a democracy. Democratic law, based on the wishes of the citizenry, attempts to balance individual freedom and the prevention of acts that infringe upon the freedom of others.

Although morality and law both relate to human conduct, they are quite different, and it is this difference that imposes the need for police or law enforcement officials. Morality is "spiritual" and not subject to man-made regulations; morality can be considered internal and law, external. If law is to create human harmony and to assure adherence to certain societal norms, there must exist machinery to effect such conduct. Law enforcement, law enforcement agencies, and the criminal justice system comprise this machinery.

⌐Generally speaking law can be categorized as *prohibitive, mandatory,* or *protective.*⌐Many laws prohibit certain

---

[1] Henry Campbell Black, *Black's Law Dictionary* (St. Paul, Minnesota: West Publishing Company, 1951), p. 1028.

actions such as killing a human being, trespassing, etc. Other laws mandate certain responsibilities of a citizen such as school attendance, registration of firearms, and licensing of motor vehicles. Still other laws provide protection that all citizens have the *right* to expect. The Bill of Rights dealing with such things as freedom of speech, trial by jury, and freedom of religion exemplifies the protective category of laws.

ORIGIN OF LAW

As this country was being settled, we adapted from England the form of custom or case law (case law referring to laws resulting from adjudged court cases). This was the origin of American law, but it certainly was not the origin of law. Actually, the legal tradition the settlers brought with them had evolved over a period of centuries and dated back to ancient times and early tribal customs. The customs of the early tribes, although not written, did constitute law as we define it, since the customs were a form of social control. Of course, in these early tribes, the chief was usually the strongest member, and it was his wish, whether contradictory or not, that often became the law of the tribe. This law may not have represented the will of the tribe, but conformance to the king's rule did, in effect, represent conformance to the law of the tribe.

As the tribes became more socialized and complex, there was an increased need for social control, and each member was required by custom, or chief's rule, to conform to certain standards of action which were conducive to the comfort of all. Eventually, the complexity of the society and customs necessitated the writing down of laws, so that all people would be aware of their responsibilities.

Hammurabi, King of Babylon around 2100 B.C., codified in writing customs deemed necessary for order and adherence to the king's rule. Hammurabi's Code is the oldest known form of written law.

The Roman occupation, the influence of Norman invaders and conquerors of the eleventh century, and the subsequent development of England all influenced the evolution of law. By the seventeenth century, the basis for English law was fairly well established in both statutory law as well as case law. It was this legal tradition that the settlers brought with them as they settled in America.

As stated earlier, although some of the law was statutory in that it was enacted by Parliament, most of it was traditional or in the form of case law. That is, it was custom or resulted from a court trial of a violation of custom.

READ ABOUT
TYPES OF LAW

To fully appreciate the significance and complexities of law and to place the police role in proper perspective, familiarity with several types of law is important. The types listed are not conclusive, but do include those which are of interest in the study of law enforcement.

As inferred previously, law can be divided into two broad general categories: 1) natural law and 2) human law.

Natural law refers to that law which is independent of enacted law or of the systems peculiar to any one society. Instead it is discoverable through man's rational intelligence and stems from his nature.[2] Natural law is a constant, unchanging concept, which exists only in pure form.

Human law often reflects natural law, but specifically refers to law that has been formally established by man. Human law, like human beings, is imperfect and does change as the needs or desires of people change.

Natural law is an abstract concept that has little or no applicability in our present diversified and complex society. Human law, however, is relevant as it is applied to indicate society's desires. Human law can be subdivided into additional categories. Of greatest significance to the law enforcement student are criminal law, civil law, common law,

[2] Henry Campbell Black, p. 1177.

10

case law, statutory law, constitutional law, and administrative law.

Criminal law deals with crimes and defines actions that are contrary to the public peace and safety. Criminal law also specifies penalties or punishment to be imposed upon offenders. Obvious examples of violations of criminal law include murder, rape, robbery, burglary, and larceny, which are concurrently called criminal acts or offenses.

Civil law is commonly considered as that law governing private relationships or disputes between private individuals concerning liability. Officially, however, civil law relates to the private rights of individuals in a community and to legal proceedings in connection with these rights. In early times civil law was the law governing the citizens of the particular governmental unit in contrast to laws applied in cases between citizens. Civil law cases are usually personal actions for the purpose of compelling payment, recovery, or redress of private and civil rights. An example of civil action would be the demand that payment be received from another person or entity responsible for personal injury. A civil case is brought to court in the form of a *suit* or a legal claim in which the plaintiff pursues the redress of an injury or the enforcement of a right.

Common law originally referred to the medieval judicial concept that law administered by the king's courts was the customary law of the kingdom. As such, common law is law derived from or based upon custom rather than enactments of a legislature. The authority of common law was derived solely from usages and customs, which the courts often recognized and confirmed. The American common law, derived from English law, has been modified with time to meet changing American needs.

Case law refers to that law which is established as the result of adjudged cases or judicial decisions. Case law involves the setting of judicial precedents, meaning that a principle of law has been declared by a court to serve as a rule for analogous cases or cases under similar circumstances. The English common law was built on precedent or became case law as a result of court action.

Statutory law refers to enacted legislation. To become law, a bill must be introduced and voted upon by a legislative body such as the Federal Congress or the law-making body of a state. Originating from elected officials, statutory law ideally represents the will of the public. Of course, this is not always true since pressure groups or powerful business enterprises often influence legislative bodies sufficiently to get special interests laws passed. The enactment of statutory law, though imperfect, is the best channel available to the public for fulfilling needs that can be satisfied by law.

Constitutional law, simply stated, is law or regulations found within the Federal and all state constitutions. Generally speaking, constitutional law refers to the judicial interpretations of such constitution. Constitutional law is very important to law enforcement because it places certain limitations on police precedures and defines individual rights that must be protected. Limitations refer to the Supreme Court's interpretation of such constitutional provisions as protection against unreasonable search and seizure, the guarantee of due process of law, and others. Constitutional law is fundamental, and no other law can supersede it or violate its principles and provisions.

Administrative law outlines the nature, duties, and responsibilities of offices or units of government. In the United States government there are laws that deal with such things as collection of the revenue, military regulations, and activities of all units of government. Police departments, like all organizations, have established administrative laws that prescribe certain responsibilities and prohibit certain activities. These are usually referred to as rules and regulations, but within an organization they have the same effect as law, often prescribing penalties for violators.

THE POLICE AND LAW

The primary responsibility of the police and most law enforcement agencies, and, in fact, the principle reason for their existence, is to enforce criminal law. In fact, the entire

12

criminal justice system exists as a result of criminal law, because the system is the mechanism for handling violations and violators.

This does not mean the police are concerned only with criminal law. Traffic regulations are not normally thought of as criminal, but the police must devote a considerable amount of their time and resources to traffic control. The police, like all law enforcement agencies, are restricted by *Constitutional* law and must be familiar with it. They must conform to *administrative* law as established by the department or the government unit which they represent. Familiarity with *civil* law is imperative because all law enforcement agencies must be able to identify it as such and must not confuse it with criminal law. In addition, the police are often called upon to describe civil law to citizens and to inform them of their rights of redress and to describe legal proceedings that can be initiated. The police must also be knowledgeable in other types of regulatory law such as licensing, building codes, and health codes so that violations can be referred to the proper enforcement agency.

LAW AND PUBLIC OPINION

From the foregoing, it is quite clear that law depends on custom, preserves custom, and generally has the approval of the people it serves. It stands, therefore, that for law to be effective, it must have general public support and must coincide with the customs, needs, and desires of society. A law that does not serve society *need not and should not be law*.

Public opinion should, and does, make laws effective or render them useless. An excellent and well-known example of this is the Eighteenth Amendment to the Constitution of the United States which prohibited the sale, manufacture, and transportation of intoxicating liquor. The unpopular law was widely and openly disobeyed until public opinion actually forced its repeal.

There are also many laws on the books, such as the Sunday "Blue Laws" (prohibiting hunting, spectator sports, retail sales, etc., on Sunday), which have lost much of their usefulness because, in light of present customs, beliefs, and desires, the need for them is not as great as it once was. As a result, these laws are ignored by both the public and the police. They are rendered useless because public opinion is not behind them.

Laws not related to present needs are not only useless, but they can be quite harmful. The police are placed in the position of having to decide which laws are beneficial to society and in turn enforcing only those. Not only is this a burden for the police, but also it places too much power in their hands, which may ultimately lead to dissension and disrespect for both the law and the police. The law should be influenced by public opinion, not the police. Useless, outmoded, and unpopular laws should be repealed by legislative bodies, and the police should enforce all laws. If law is to serve the public, it must relate to their needs, desires, demands, and it must be enforced by the police.

This advocacy of societal control of law should not infer justification of disobedience to the law. If we recognize and accept the need for law, we must also be willing to accept the consequences resulting from disobedience of the law. No matter how justified the cause, civil disobedience is a violation of the law, and prescribed punishment should be administered. More emphatically, *violence in protesting a law is never justified*. The society should cause the repeal or modification of undesirable laws, but such changes should result from lawful processes such as voting or peaceful persuasion.

POLICE AUTHORITY

In the context of this book, police authority is synonymous with the term police power as both relate to the legal authority for having police and for establishing law enforcement agencies.

In countries like England and France, it is relatively

14

simple to identify the legal basis of police authority because law enforcement operates under a centralized government and all police are under national control. In the United States, with government fragmented into various jurisdictional levels and geographical divisions, there is no general "police authority" law; we must refer to the laws and ordinances of the many jurisdictional units of government: national, state, county, and municipal.

The laws pertaining to police and police authority become particularly confusing at the local level because many states have various classes of municipalities, each with its own regulations governing the police. For example, Pennsylvania local governments are classed as boroughs; townships of the first, second, and third class; and cities of the first, second, and third class. There are state laws pertaining to police authority that are general to all local governments. Confusing, however, are additional state laws that are peculiar to each category of local government and that very frequently differ from each other.

At the risk of inaccuracy due to oversimplification, the general statement may be made that the sources of the law controlling police agencies fall into three main divisions:

Know

1. The Federal Constitution, related statutes, and judicial decisions outline the powers, duties, and limitations of the national police agencies.
2. The state constitutions, related statutes, and judicial decisions outline the legal rights, duties, and powers of the police officer; establish the nature of his office; and govern the organization and administration of state police agencies and state controlled municipal police departments.
3. In general, municipal charters and ordinances govern the organization, administration, and operations of municipal police departments.

There are numerous exceptions to these generalities, but it is relatively safe to think in terms of such divisions when discussing police authority in general.

15

FEDERAL LAW ENFORCEMENT

The Federal Constitution has no specific provision for the existence of law enforcement agencies at the federal, state, or local level of government. Therefore, by virtue of the Tenth Amendment to the United States Constitution, such power is reserved to the states. Because of the Tenth Amendment, we can say that the primary source for police authority is the state.

The Federal Congress does, however, have the implied police power which authorizes the establishment of law enforcement agencies to carry out their responsibilities as outlined by the Constitution. Even though the Constitution does not specifically provide for federal law enforcement agencies, Congress can establish such agencies in order to execute or enforce the provisions of the Constitution. This implied power is derived from Article I, Section 8, of the Constitution which states:

> To make all laws which shall be necessary and proper for carrying into execution the foregoing powers, vested by this Constitution in the Government of the United States, or in any Department or officer thereof.

Therefore, since Article I, Section 8, of the Constitution established the power to coin money and punish counterfeiters, Congress was legally able to establish the Secret Service for investigative and enforcement purposes. Like the Secret Service, all other federal law enforcement agencies have evolved from the same police authority basis.

Other Articles deal more specifically with the authority to enforce provisions of the Constitution. For example, Article XIII, Section 2, reads, "Congress shall have power to enforce this article by appropriate legislation." Article XIV, Section 5, reads, "The Congress shall have power to enforce by appropriate legislation, the provisions of this article." Generally, however, the authority to establish federal law enforcement agencies is based on the implied power in Article I, Section 8, Paragraph 18. The Alcohol and Tobacco Tax Division was established to enforce liquor tax violations, tobacco tax violations, and the National Firearms Act. The Federal Bureau of Narcotics was established to supervise the laws governing narcotics, etc.

STATE POLICE AUTHORITY

As indicated previously, the states possess primary police authority and have established the police systems within the states. Normally, each state has created or allowed for the creation of municipal police departments for cities and sheriffs to enforce the law in the rural areas. When doing this, the state constitution or state law usually defines a police officer, outlines his powers and duties, and imposes constitutional limitations on the office. Beyond this, the state usually reserves the power of administration, organization, and operations to the local government.

There are, however, several exceptions to this rule of local control, and some states do impose strict supervision upon local police agencies. Additionally, those states that did not originally retain some supervisory control have subsequently passed legislation doing just that. A recent trend, for example, has been the passage of state legislation requiring minimum standards for selection, training, or education of local police officers. Such state control not only forces improvement but also usually provides the necessary resources for improvement.

The state, of course, also has the power to establish state police agencies and to pass legislation pertaining to the operation, management, organization, and supervision of such agencies. Some states have established state police agencies which practice full police powers throughout the rural areas of the state. Other states have established highway patrols and have made county government responsible for general policing of the rural areas. In both situations, municipalities have the responsibility for enforcement of the law within their jurisdiction.

States have also established special law enforcement agencies to enforce specific laws and to assist local law en-

17

forcement. Many states, for example, have agencies for enforcing narcotics violations, liquor violations, etc. Many states, especially those with highway patrols, have an organized criminal investigation division to enforce state laws and to assist local law enforcement.

LOCAL POLICE AUTHORITY

As mentioned previously, authority for the existence of local police agencies is found in individual state constitutions. While the state constructs the framework within which local police can exist, the local government establishes operational procedures and administration.

Some states exercise more control than others, but usually the local police officer is in reality a state officer because he derives his authority from the state. Many city or county charters detail precisely police powers and responsibilities, but in actuality the local charters merely restate or clarify the state constitution and related statutes.

Although actual operation is usually under local control, there are some cities that are directly under state control. Among such cities are St. Louis and Baltimore. Even then, however, the degree of control varies from city to city and from state to state.

LEGAL RESTRICTIONS

Police authority or power is reserved to the states, and the authority to establish federal law enforcement agencies is implied to Congress in the United States Constitution. However, such authority is not unlimited or without safeguards. Our forefathers were very concerned about the possible development of a "police state," and so certain undeniable rights of all citizens were placed in the original ten amendments to the Constitution, more commonly known as the Bill of Rights.

The Bill of Rights and related judicial decisions do limit police authority and do protect citizens against the possibil-

18

ity of a "police state." In addition, subsequent legislation has established additional civil rights which define or guarantee certain freedoms for all citizens.

Police power and action cannot conflict with the rights of the individual. Individual fundamental rights include such liberties as freedom of religion, speech, press, assembly, and petition; right to bear arms; due process of law; speedy jury trial; indictment only by grand jury; no excessive bail or fine; no cruel or unusual punishment; no double jeopardy by retrial for the same offense; and the right of the people to be secure in their persons, houses, papers, and effects against unreasonable searches and seizures.

Summary

The enforcement of the law is one of the most influential mechanisms for social control in existence. Yet, inconsistent with its significance, law enforcement remains a subject that the public knows less about than any other governmental function.

Though the concept of law enforcement is most visibly manifested in the presence of the law enforcement or police officer, there are other agencies involved in crime control and the maintenance of order. These agencies are referred to collectively as the "criminal justice system." This system has three separately organized units consisting of the police, courts, and corrections. Generally speaking, the police are charged with the detection, identification, and apprehension of law violators; courts hear cases, weigh evidence, interpret law, and determine guilt or innocence; and corrections is charged with detention and rehabilitation of the offender.

The entire criminal justice system evolved as a result of law, and its existence is controlled and directed by law. Law is essential to society and forms the basis of a democracy. Democratic law, based on the wishes of the citizenry, attempts to balance individual freedom and the prevention of acts that infringe upon the freedom of others.

Law can be divided into two broad general categories: 1) natural law and 2) human law. Human law is of concern in law enforcement, and types of human law include criminal law, civil law, common law, case law, statutory law, and administrative law. The type of law of most concern to the police is criminal law and, in fact, the entire criminal justice system exists as a result of criminal law.

The authority for the existence of local and state police generally is contained in state constitutions, since the Federal Constitution makes no provision for the existence of law enforcement agencies. Federal police agencies have been established by the implied police power granted by the Constitution which authorizes the establishment of law enforcement agencies to carry out the responsibilities assigned Congress.

20

Discussion Questions

1. What is the role of law enforcement in our democratic society?
2. Define law enforcement and the criminal justice system.
3. What are the responsibilities of each unit of the criminal justice system?
4. Why does the criminal justice system owe its existence to law?
5. What are the different types of law?
6. What purpose does law serve?
7. What types of law are of concern to the police?
8. What is the relationship between law and public opinion?
9. How do the police derive their authority?
10. What legal restrictions are imposed upon the police?

2

Development of
American Law Enforcement

Law enforcement as we know it today has its roots within the mysterious past. Law enforcement agencies evolved slowly throughout ancient, medieval, and modern history in response to the social needs of an ever-advancing civilization.

Understanding of the continuous but often haphazard development of law enforcement is important since it provides an indepth appreciation of the police role and function in modern society. Familiarity with the history of law enforcement helps emphasize that law enforcement came into existence as a social need and, concurrently, as a social function. Just as law enforcement evolved in response to past social needs, it is presently changing to meet changing social needs. Knowledge of the history of law enforcement is important because an understanding of its early development helps us to better understand and appreciate present changes.

A deep appreciation for the law enforcement heritage will also instill a feeling of pride in the profession and in its recent accomplishments. Such pride will enhance law enforcement and place it in proper perspective with other academic and professional disciplines.

ANCIENT HISTORY OF LAW ENFORCEMENT (TO 500 A.D.)

EARLY TRIBAL LIFE

There is ample historical evidence to indicate that a form of law enforcement was familiar even to early tribal people. Of course, people at that time did not employ enforcement as we understand it, but for all general purposes they were involved in the principle of law enforcement. Archaeological findings such as cave drawings and early tablets give evidence that tribes were concerned with protection and the enforcement of social codes. Most needs were based on survival, but the concept of protection from marauders and each other can certainly be related to a form of policing.

Many ancient tribes probably looked to their chief for protection and the preservation of social order. As such, the chief's doctrines or commands were obeyed for fear of admonishment or even punishment. In this sense, the chief established law, enforced law, and also adjudicated law.

As ancient society became more complex, additional rules of conduct had to be established to promote harmony. Concurrent with the increasing size and complexity of society, it became more difficult to administer tribal custom. As a result, the chief probably designated certain individuals or groups of individuals to seek violators and bring them before him. In a sense, these military aids were law enforcement officers. Of course, the rules laid down by tribal leaders were not laws as such but were customs which law later reflected.

Law enforcement developed concurrently with law, since law had to exist before it could be enforced. In other words, enforcement methods were developed in order to achieve conformance to the emerging body of law.

FORMALIZED LAW

The existence of formal law and, therefore, the concept of law enforcement can be traced to ancient Babylon. There is archaeological proof that 2,000 years before the birth of Christ, Hammurabi, King of Babylon, compiled a legal code dealing with such things as commercial law, land law, and criminal law. More specifically, the laws dealt with such things as responsibilities of the individual to the group and private dealings between individuals. There were also provisions of penalties of the retributive type exemplifying the "lex talionis" or the law of the talon. Messengers were referred to as those responsible for carrying out the law.

The Old Testament also contains many provisions of law or customs relating to property, inheritance, slaves, and even crime. Of course, these provisions reflected highly religious principles rather than just the needs of society. The enforcement of such principles was obviously the responsibility of the religious leaders or their representatives rather than of organized police forces.

GREEK INFLUENCE

Near Eastern civilizations also contributed to the development of law and law enforcement. However, the real influence occurred with modification and solidification of law by the Greeks and, ultimately, the Romans.

The early Greek city-states witnessed considerable turmoil during their existence. Much of the citizen unrest resulted from a strife between powerful groups. At various stages, rulership was intermittently rotated between a king, the wealthy merchants, and participation by free citizens. It is significant that in every case rules were established to meet the needs as understood by those in control and adherence was then enforced by military units.

Eventually, as a result of continuous wars, the city-states declined and huge kingdoms came into existence. Kings ruled and carefully controlled the lives of the people. Again, a sort of military police enforced the rules of the king.

The early Greek city-states did, however, witness some development from tribal policing to more formalized policing. For example, Pisistratus (605–527 B.C.), an early ruler of Athens, established a guard system. The responsibilities of these guards included the protection of the tower, highways, and their ruler.

Solon (639–559 B.C.) probably contributed more to the development of law enforcement than any previous leader had. Solon ruled Athens democratically and devised a system by which a general assembly of freemen passed the laws, and instituted courts in which the jury was chosen from the citizenry. On the other hand, the rulers of Sparta, the other great city-state, were completely authoritarian and personally controlled matters of justice.

ROMAN INFLUENCE

During their period of expansion, the Romans finally conquered the entire Mediterranean world. Rome imposed on the newly absorbed Greek culture its own law and organization. In doing so, the Romans had considerable influence on the development of law enforcement. The Roman's attempt to secure justice for all people was reflected in its body of law referred to as *the twelve tables* which related to such things as judicial process, ownership, inheritance, and torts. (Tort refers to willful or negligent injury to an individual's person, property, or reputation.) Magistrates were appointed to adjudicate, but they were given or assumed great latitude in exercising their powers and in laying down decisions.

Perhaps the greatest Roman contributor to law enforcement was Caius Julius Caesar Octavianus (Octavian). He was the grandnephew and heir of Julius Caesar. In 27 B.C., the Senate decreed that his name should be Augustus which meant *exalted* or *consecrated*.

Augustus (63 B.C.–14 A.D.) utilized a military unit called a *cohort* to serve as his army and to protect the city. A cohort was comprised of from 500 to 1000 men, and three such cohorts were assigned to the city of Rome. The soldiers of a cohort were called *praetorians*, and these praetorians were scattered throughout Rome and were probably dressed as civilians. Civilian dress was in response to the resistance to military control and was a means of disguising the praetorians as civilians.

The many large-scale disorders in Rome during the reign of Augustus evidenced the inadequacy of existing local law enforcement and forced Augustus to improve the system.

28

Originally, slaves under the supervision of an appointed official were expected to quell riots and disorders. Not only did this system prove totally inadequate, but also its inefficiency actually contributed to the disorder.

The praetorian guard was considered an elite group in Roman society and, therefore, Augustus was reluctant to ask it to function as riot police. As an alternative, he established the *urban cohort*. Members of both groups were selected from the military units, but standards for the praetorian guard were somewhat higher than those for the urban cohort. The urban cohort had the specific responsibilities of keeping order among the slaves and of controlling unruly citizens.

Part of Roman disorder was reflected in the devastating fires that occurred throughout the city. As he had done with riots, Augustus originally expected large groups of slaves under the direction of an appointed official to extinguish fires. The use of slaves proved totally inadequate again and finally Augustus established the *vigiles of Rome*. Rather than have this new unit assume just the fire-fighting responsibility, he also assigned them the task of policing, which was previously carried out by the urban cohort. In this sense, we see the establishment of the first *police-fire integrated service*. Their function was to control fires and to exercise police functions which included the right to arrest thieves and housebreakers as well as to control and suppress riots.

The vigiles of Rome were not selected from the military legions, and were, therefore, the first nonmilitary or civilian police force. We also see the direct implementation of home rule, because the vigiles consisted of freemen appointed to serve in that capacity. Of course, this may be also the origin of the patronage system which still plagues many police departments. (Patronage is the appointment of people to jobs as a reward for their previous favors.)

Another contribution of Augustus was his organization of the city into *wards* to facilitate the operation of government which included the police function. Such decentralization was necessary not only for organizational control, but also to reduce response time in the event of disorder. Groups of vigiles were assigned to the various wards, and we see the emergence of the police administrative concept, *division by area.* The *ward system* was used throughout the early development of law enforcement, and this concept is still common to modern law enforcement. Today, however, we commonly refer to such a division as a *precinct* rather than a ward.

A later Roman contributor to law enforcement was the Byzantine emperor Justinian (483–565 A.D.) who summarized the Roman law into what is known as *corpus juris civilis* or body of civil law. This is probably the world's most famous and influential law book. Roman law more or less contributed to the concepts of fair trial, proof of guilt, and opportunity of accused to meet his accuser.

ANCIENT PUNISHMENT

As might be expected, ancient punishment was usually quite crude, cruel, and often consisted of the infliction of pain upon the offender. In early societies, offenses were often left to the family or clan group to settle as they saw fit. As a result, the degree and kind of punishment were dependent upon the personality and strength of the person or group offended, since they were the executors. In fact, it was quite common for one clan to seek retaliatory compensation from the entire clan to which the offender belonged. The practice contributed to the beginning of the so-called family or *blood feuds* since the right of one clan to punish the other was not necessarily limited to the punishment of the individual that actually committed the offense.

As defined in the Laws of Hammurabi, ancient society held to the belief of *lex talionis* which implies *an eye for an eye* or *a tooth for a tooth.* If a person inflicted a particular injury upon another individual, the retaliatory punishment would be the infliction of the same injury upon the accused.

As society developed, certain punishments became customary for certain offenses. If a person stole, for example, he might have been punished by having his hand amputated or by some other predetermined mandate. Ancient punishment may have included such things as mutilation, partial dismemberment of the body, exposure to wild beasts, burning at the stake, and stoning to death.

ENGLISH DEVELOPMENT DURING MEDIEVAL HISTORY (500 A.D.–1500 A.D.)

ANGLO-SAXON ENGLAND

The collapse of the Roman conquest of England was followed by several hundred years of confusion and increasing barbarism. Finally, during the fifth and sixth centuries, the Angles and Saxons became conquerors and settlers rather than just marauders. They brought governmental organization to England and with it the development of local law enforcement. Policing, for the most part, was delegated to the people on the basis of mutual responsibility. The king's peace was actually the promise of protection, peace, and security to the people in return for their allegiance.

King Alfred (872–901) one of the most influential Anglo-Saxon kings, held landed proprietors responsible for the members of their household. Alfred devoted considerable energy to the task of preserving peace within his kingdom. One of Alfred's contributions was a new body of law or *dooms* which covered a variety of subjects. His code included such provisions as the declaration of forms of punishment and the sums an offender was to be fined for committing an offense.

The customs, government, and divisions of England evolved and became firmly established during Alfred's reign. This period profoundly influenced the subsequent development of law enforcement.

Organizational structure. Most of the people of Anglo-Saxon England lived in villages, which were known as *tuns* from which we derive our word *town*. In the tun, law enforcement was everyone's responsibility. When an offense was committed, a *hue and cry* was issued, and every able-bodied man was required to take chase or help in the apprehension of the offender. In a sense, this practice represents the first use of the *citizen's arrest*. As in earlier times, when a member of one tun committed an offense against the other tun, subsequent action was retaliatory in nature. Each tun was responsible for the actions of its members and was, therefore, punishable as an entity.

As tuns became larger and more complex, it became necessary to subdivide them into *tithings*. The tithing consisted of ten families, and responsibility for protecting the tun and maintaining peace among the tun's people was rotated among the tithings. Each tithing was held responsible for the conduct of its members and if a member committed an offense, the tithing had to make retribution. One member of the tithing was elected by the group and was called the *chief tithingman*. When his tithing was providing police services, he had the responsibility of raising the hue and cry and for executing punishment when an offender was apprehended and found guilty.

A group of ten tithings, called a *hundred*, comprised the framework for accomplishing judicial work. The *hundred's court* was responsible for rendering punishments, settling land disputes, and settling disputes between groups within the hundred. The head man of the hundred was called the *reeve*. Although the king could intervene, the people generally handled disputes among and between themselves. Thus, again we see the evolution of community or local rule. It is interesting, too, that cases could be appealed to the king for settlement.

A larger geographical unit comprised of several hundreds was the *shire*. The shire was governed by an *ealdorman* who was appointed by the king or by one of the king's royal officers. An ealdorman was usually a great noble who owned extensive lands in the part of the country he governed. He was sort of a governor and, when necessary, had the power to call out the fighting force of the shire. Eventually, the ealdorman became know as the *earl*, which is a more common usage today.

The ealdorman did not, however, have complete control and authority over his shire. The king appointed a *shire-reeve* and subsequently looked upon this office as the primary liaison between the crown and the shire. The word sheriff is derived from shire-reeve and to some extent our present office of sheriff is similar to the early office of the shire-reeve. The shire-reeve had the assigned responsibilities of collecting taxes, enforcing law, and attending to all affairs of the government as viewed necessary by the king. He had the power of *posse comitatus* which allowed him to command able-bodied men of the shire to offer assistance. The shire-reeve was the king's official representative, and it was natural that he became even more powerful than the ealdorman, and eventually he became one of the most powerful political figures of the time.

This tithing system of Anglo-Saxon England can be logically compared with our present day police system which includes local police, county police, and state police. Our courts are also organized under a similar arrangement, including appeal to the federal court.

Justice. From time to time the landowners and other official men of the shire would meet to discuss and resolve a variety of problems. In addition to regular business, messages from the king were announced, and lawsuits were often settled. These meetings were referred to as the *hundred's courts, shire courts,* or the *hundred* or *shire mote*.

When a person was charged with an offense within the hundred or shire, there were generally two customary methods of determining his guilt or innocence. They were the *oath* and the *ordeal*. Both were based on the premise of an appeal to God asking him to indicate which person was telling the truth.

The oath required several people known as *compurgators* to testify relative to another's innocence or veracity. The accused would furnish a certain number of compurgators and each would then take a solemn oath that the accused was telling the truth. Evidence or the compurgator's knowledge of the event was not important as long as he would support the oath of the accused. Actually, the compurgator was a character witness and, customary to the times, the value of his support became greater if he held a high social rank or position. In other words, oaths of such men were of much greater value than the oaths of men who held a lower status in the society.

In the absence of compurgators, the courts could demand *trial by ordeal*. For example, the accused would be required to carry a red hot iron in his bare hand for a specified distance. His hand would then be bandaged for a specified length of time. Upon removing the bandages, the person was deemed innocent if by divine help the hand was healed and guilty if the hand was not healed.

Ordeal by water consisted of appropriate prayers, binding the accused with rope, and then throwing him into a body of water. If he was received by the water and sank, he was deemed innocent. If, on the other hand, the water rejected him and he floated, he was deemed guilty. In either event, the accused was quickly retrieved from the water and released or punished accordingly.

Actually, this primitive trial process was not entirely unsuccessful. Certainly the fear of ordeal led many offenders to confess their sins and admit guilt. Obviously, however, many innocent people were declared guilty or confessed to something they didn't do rather than face the ordeal. Regardless of their system's inadequacies, it is important to realize that the Anglo-Saxons were interested in achieving justice, otherwise they would not have devised any method for determining guilt. Perhaps they realized the human inability to devise a system that would achieve *true justice* and thus turned to God for wisdom and power.

Capital punishment was seldom used, but branding was quite common. Branding, however, may have been more for identification of criminals rather than for punishment. The most common form of punishment was the payment of fines. Punishment was graduated to fit the crime and depended upon the position or class of the victim. As a result, a very elaborate system of fines was developed. The more severe the crime committed, the higher the fine became. At the same time, if the position or class of the victim was high, the fine would be higher than if the victim was from a lower class. The complexity of the system is illustrated in King Alfred's *dooms*. It states, for example, that a man stabbed in the thigh will receive thirty shillings from the perpetrator. A specified amount was even payable by a murderer or his family to the family of the victim.

NORMAN INFLUENCE

In 1066, William the Conqueror invaded and conquered England. William and his predecessors had an uncanny genius for government that the Anglo-Saxons did not possess. Whereas the Anglo-Saxons were committed to local government, the Normans were more interested in national control and established a highly formal centralized bureaucracy, which unified the country's law enforcement processes.

King William (1027–1087), known as William the Conqueror, maintained the same organization of shires and hundreds but appointed his own sheriffs of the shires, or counties as the shires came to be known. At the same time, he strengthened the positions of county officials and formalized centralized control. Within a very few years Norman earls, sheriffs, barons, and knights superseded the Saxon earls and shire-reeves in official positions and as landowners.

William introduced harsh *forest laws*, under which large tracts of forest were preserved for deer hunting by the King and his nobles exclusively. The severe punishment meted out to violators of these laws caused historians to judge William's reign as tyrannical.

William also introduced the concept of a *curfew*, which required that all fires be extinguished or covered at nightfall.

In the judicial system, William added to the previously developed concepts of trial by oath and by ordeal the concept of *wager of battle* or *trial by combat*. If one man charged another with an offense, the court would determine the truth on the basis of the resulting battle between the accused and the accuser. The person winning the battle was deemed in the right and the person losing was deemed to be in the wrong.

The *doomsday book* was another legal contribution of William. This book was essentially a tax roll listing the landowners and the extent of their lands. It is significant of his great authority that William was able to compel the people of England to give the kind of information that people even today frequently decline or hesitate to give census takers. His ability to put these reports into order also illustrates the establishment of a very efficient and well-organized body of government officials.

Henry I and Legis Henrici (1100–1135). The next Norman king who significantly influenced the development of law enforcement was William's younger brother, Henry I. In fact, Henry's contributions were so pertinent that he became known as the *lawgiver*. This title was primarily a result of his issuance of the *legis henrici* which established certain offenses, such as arson, robbery, murder, false coinage, and crimes of violence, as being against the king's peace. Thus, emerged the concept of *disturbance of the peace* and the idea that a person should be punished by the state rather than by the victim or his group. The legis henrici also differentiated crimes as being either *felonies or misdemeanors*—divisions we use today. Murder, robbery, arson, and other violent crimes were felonious, while crimes of a lesser nature were misdemeanors.

Recognizing that many lawsuits could be tried satisfactorily only in the area where the matters at issue were known, Henry established roving or traveling justices. These royal justices became known as *circuit justices* because they were sent throughout the established regular circuits. This custom of circuit judges has been customary in England ever since and was utilized also in the early American West.

ANGEVIN RULE (1154–1399)

It was during the reigns of the seven Angevin kings that the foundations of national unity were laid in England. During this period laws were further strengthened, and the processes of justice were more definitely established. This period is called Angevin in recognition of Henry II, the first of the line that reigned for nearly 245 years. Henry II was one of the most able of all the English kings, and he initiated the many reforms that led to national unity such as had not been enjoyed since Alfred.

Henry II and trial by jury (1154–1188). The reign of Henry I was followed by many years of strife and turmoil that did not end until Henry II came into power. Henry II's greatest contribution to the development of law enforcement was the foundation he laid for the jury system. Henry II reinstated the circuit justices of Henry I and at the same time improved and extended them. We see during Henry II's reign, for example, the origin of *trial by jury*. The king's justices used a new form of trial rather than by ordeal, compurgation, or wager of battle. They called this an *inquisition*. At the inquisition, persons were required to give information under oath on any matters requested of them by the justices. When asked to hear a case, the judges would order a number of men, usually twelve, to investigate the case and give a sworn *verdict* as to which of the people had the better right in the dispute. These selected men were known as *jurors* because they had to swear to tell the truth and were required to decide in favor of one or the other of the people involved in the case. Thus, we see the beginning of trial by jury, the jurors being peers of the defendant.

The origin of indictment by jury can also be attributed to the reign of Henry II. He issued the *assize of Clarendon*, the object of which was to introduce a reform in the punishment of crimes. It provided that when the king's justices came to the hundred's mote, twelve men from each hundred and four men from each manor in the hundred would be put upon their oath and required to give the names of any men they knew who had been accused or suspected of having committed a great crime. This allowed for the punishment of all persons committing an offense rather than of just those persons that may have been reported to the sheriff.

It was during Henry II's reign also that justices began to keep a record of the cases settled and the decisions that were given. The justices were educated men and their decisions were given on principles that were quite logical, consistent, and in comformance with the customs then existing. These decisions as laid down by the king's justices became known as *common law*. The recording of decisions based upon precedent did much to bring about conformity and uniformity in both national law and customs of the age.

The church. During this period, the church had attained practically as much power as the government. The church was so powerful that it was actually immune from normal law enforcement practices to the extent that it had its own courts to try cases concerning the clergy. These church courts had been important ever since the early Norman conquest, and it was William I who stipulated that church matters should be tried by the bishops in courts of their own rather than in hundred and shire courts. The church stipulated that all cases involving clergymen, church property, marriages, wills, inheritance, and those involving a breach of an oath should be heard by the church. Thus, we see the inauguration of *benefit of clergy*, which exempted clergy from trial or punishment except through a church court. We also see the custom of *sanctuary* that provided the fugitive from justice with immunity from arrest or apprehension if he were in a church.

The evolution of such protections is easily understood when one considers the types of punishment issued by the other courts. For example, capital punishment consisted of

38

beheading or hanging to strangulation, being buried alive, boiling, and impaling. Lesser punishments consisted of such things as the pillory, whipping, the rack, the wheel, and the strappado.

King John and the Great Charter (1199–1216). Although King John is known as one of the worst kings of English history, his seventeen-year reign did contribute to the development of law enforcement. Because of his oppressive actions and heavy taxation, he was completely disliked by both the people and his nobles. King John imposed increasingly greater taxes upon the people and demanded that the barons fulfill military services. However, he did not lead them to war but kept them waiting until they were willing to pay a fee to go home. He even used the courts to plunder the clergy. In addition to the oppressions, the king was hateful to so many that a rebellion against him was unavoidable. Finally, as a result of pressures from the church, the noblemen and the general populace, King John gave way and signed the *Great Charter* at Runnymeade on June 15, 1215. He granted the list of demands by the church, the barons, and those drawn up by townsmen. This charter became known as the *Magna Carta* and is one of the most notable documents in history. The Magna Carta is of particular importance to law enforcement because local control was restored, trial by jury was assured, and due process of law was installed as a right of all people. These guarantees were of such importance that they are also reflected in the fifth and sixth amendments of the Constitution of the United States.

The importance of the Magna Carta relative to the democratic philosophy was illustrated quite aptly by England and her memorial to the late President John F. Kennedy. In 1965, England set aside one acre of land to be known as Runnymeade, U.S.A. By this move, one acre of English land became the property of the United States.

King Edward I and the Statute of Winchester (1274–1307). King Edward I so greatly influenced the course of events relative to law enforcement that in this respect he can be considered the equal to Augustus. Edward I probably contributed more to legal reform and law enforcement than any person preceding him.

As a result of the increasing frequency of robberies, murders, and arsons, coupled with the reluctance of officials to arrest and prosecute, Edward issued the *Statute of Winchester*. Juries were not suppressing crime, and citizens were reluctant to convict each other or were afraid of retaliation if they accused the lords. Edward's statute dealt with this problem by making it illegal for people to conceal committed felonies or to harbor felons.

The Statute of Winchester also required that the hue and cry be raised when felonies or cimes were committed in counties, hundreds, markets, fairs, or any place where a large number of people were grouped. The statute further stipulated that ignorance of the law was no excuse, and that every county had to be efficiently governed. In conjunction with this, when a felony was committed, immediate pursuit was required that would continue from town to town and county to county until the offender was apprehended.

Of great importance to local control was a provision that held people dwelling in the county answerable for robberies and resulting damages within their area. Local responsibility was demanded, in that the whole hundred where a robbery was committed was liable for the crime. This gave additional impetus for local policing since the people of the hundred needed a means to prevent crimes now that they were held responsible.

Other provisions required large towns with walls to close their gates at night and forbade persons from lodging in the suburbs or near the town except during the daytime and only then if a host vouched for him. From this evolved our concept of vagrancy and loitering laws. *Bailiffs* were mentioned as having the responsibility of checking for such people and taking appropriate action.

Watches were required to be assigned to the gate of every borough or town within the country. The statute was so specific as to say that every city would have six men at every gate, every borough would assign twelve men, and every town, six or four depending on its population. Strangers were to be arrested and delivered to the sheriff. The *night watchmen* or *bailiffs* were selected from the ranks of able-bodied citizens within the community and were required to serve but were paid for their services. On some watches, the watchmen grouped themselves together and roamed throughout the city thus forming a *marching watch* which may very well have been the first known patrol activity of a law enforcement agency. Another unique characteristic of the night watch was the eventual addition of a specialized police unit called *police des mouers* that was responsible for regulating prostitutes throughout the cities.

Another provision of the statute required that highways leading from one market town to another be cleared to a width of two hundred feet on each side so there was no place of concealment for criminals. Landlords were required to clear the roads on their land and if they did not, they were held responsible for crimes committed and required to pay a fine to the king.

The Statute of Winchester also commanded that every able-bodied man arm himself to the degree that his station in life allowed. Such ability, of course, ranged from the most sophisticated of weapons possessed by the richer people to the least sophisticated of weapons available to the poor people. To initiate control over this army, the king stipulated that weapons be inspected two times every two years and that every hundred assign two *constables* to handle and inspect the weapons.

Other reforms of Edward I dealt with offenses of royal servants, forbade the corrupt maintenance of lawsuits by judges or sheriffs, and ordered free elections. In an attempt to bring reform in the justice system, Edward more than once replaced all of the sheriffs, removed many judges from the bench, and accused nearly eight hundred officials. These events actually were forerunners to the establishment of a *justice of the peace* who was to supersede the sheriff.

The reign of Edward I marked a definite trend in the history of common law. Previously, law had been flexible and judges used wide and varying discretion when making decisions. Now law was developing from the decisions of justices and from new writs issued by the chancellor. Edward's statutes gave law order and organization and at the same time made it more rigid. This rigidity actually paved the way for equity in the laws of the land, replacing arbitrary decisions by justices.

Edward III and justices of the peace (1327–1377). Under Edward III, justices of the peace were appointed to assist itinerant justices, to help maintain the peace, and even to try cases themselves. The office of sheriff still existed but the justice of the peace took over much of the sheriff's former responsibilities, and in time became much more powerful than the sheriff. The justice of the peace could punish petty offenses brought to his attention by an accuser, a constable, or the policemen of the village. He could punish drunkenness or card playing on the sabbath or the refusal to work at harvest time. He could order a vagabond whipped. He could force suspected persons to give bond to keep the peace or appear in court, or he could hold them in jail until they were tried. It was his duty to stop a riot before it became dangerous although he could not punish the rioters.

Edward III's act relative to the justice of the peace actually combined in that office the police function with the function of a judge. In fact, the justice of the peace had the power to inquire into the activities of sheriffs and punish them if they had violated the law.

Justices of the peace, who were usually country gentlemen, were required to be learned in the law since such knowledge was deemed necessary to carry out their responsibilities. We, therefore, see the emergence of the belief that in order to fulfill their responsibilities, police officers must be competent and trained.

King Edward III also issued the *Statutes of Treason* which made giving aid and comfort to enemies of the land

42

the offense of treason. The same statute also contained provisions against counterfeiting and indicated that those engaged in such activity were also guilty of treason.

DEVELOPMENT OF ENGLISH LAW ENFORCEMENT DURING EARLY MODERN HISTORY (FROM 1500)

The reign of King Charles I (1625–1645) was marked by his constant dispute with Parliament and by his belligerent attitude toward Parliament and its members. Because Parliament would not provide him with funds, Charles initiated illegal actions and forced loans which created great resentment on the part of Parliament and lords of the day. Charles totally ignored Parliament and all previous rights afforded the people by past rulers. He tried to operate on the basis of absolute rule by the king.

Court of Star Chamber. In conjunction with his high-handed methods, Charles forced compliance by the subversive use of the *Court of Star Chamber* which was actually instituted by Henry VII in 1487 for the purpose of trying special cases such as bribing sheriffs or jurymen. The members of the court were appointed by the king, and, in reality, the court was a means by which the king could demand his will while under the disguise of judicial authority.

The court charged persons, and then the same body heard the case and pronounced sentence. The court called witnesses but did not allow the defendant to be represented or to present his case. Actually, to be charged by the court was the same as being condemned.

In reaching their preconceived decisions the high justices frequently resorted to the *third degree* or torture to induce a confession. Obviously, many defendants would confess rather than suffer continuous third-degree tactics. The court could find the accused guilty without the confession, but securing it probably made the judicial process seem more legitimate. In essence, the Court of Star Chamber by virtue of its authority derived from the king was a form of *legalized third degree*. The court enjoyed complete freedom to try cases arbitrarily and was not committed to limitations imposed upon other judicial systems or processes.

The court also imposed cruel punishments which often consisted of heavy fines, flogging, the pillory, imprisonment, and the cutting off of the ears of the convicted person. For example, a lawyer by the name of William Prynne was charged with libel because a book he had written charged sinfulness in drama. Charles enjoyed the theatre and saw this as a reflection upon his character. Prynne was, therefore, charged with libel, convicted, and sentenced to the pillory, loss of ears, fined five thousand pounds, and imprisoned until the king would wish to release him.

In reality, the Court of Star Chamber was exploited by Charles and was a threat by which he could demand his will while under the auspice of the court. Men would yield to his demands rather than face certain conviction and harsh punishment by the court. Charles was achieving forced cooperation by using the Court of Star Chamber as a tool which instilled fear of judicial retaliation if demands were not met.

Petition of Rights. In 1628, the problems between Parliament and Charles came to a head when Parliament refused to grant revenue to Charles until he signed the "Petition of Right." This petition was intended to end Charles' complete disregard for Parliament and his illegal activities. Actually, this document reaffirmed many of the provisions of previous concessions agreed to by former kings. For example, many of its provisions were a repeat of agreements found in the Magna Carta signed by King John in 1215.

The Petition of Rights specifically stated that no man could be compelled to make loans to the king against his will, to give gifts, or pay any tax not stipulated by Parliament. It also provided that freemen could not be imprisoned or detained without observance of the law and the land and without due process of law. This petition again indicated that the will of the people was above that of the king and, therefore, gave local control back to the people.

Charles signed the document but had no intention of abiding by it. He continued his devious methods and utilized the Court of Star Chamber even more. Finally, demands were such that, along with other constitutional reforms, Charles was forced to sign a measure in 1641 that abolished the Court of Star Chamber.

Finally, as a result of his tyrannical methods, civil war broke. Charles was finally beaten, tried, and was beheaded in 1649.

OLIVER CROMWELL AND MILITARY RULE (1653–1658)

Following the execution of Charles, Oliver Cromwell assumed leadership of the country under military rule. Cromwell was a good administrator who managed to raise England to a position of international prominence while maintaining law and order. For all purposes, Cromwell was king, but he refused the title and became known as *Lord Protector* instead. The country was divided into twelve districts and a general or *provost marshal* was placed at the head of each. The provost marshals held arbitrary powers in enforcing the law.

Although law and order was maintained successfully under martial law, the techniques involved total political suppression. The people resented the power of the army and their rule by a dictator. This attitude was reflected in the desire for safeguards against military rule carried to America by the English settlers.

It must be remembered, however, that he was able to keep peace and order in England which was a demoralized state. Perhaps, due to the chaotic problems, this was about the only means available for controlling crime and disorder.

KING CHARLES II AND HABEAS CORPUS (1660–1684)

Following Cromwell's death in 1658, his son became protector for a short time, but due to his inability, Parliament asked Charles II, son of Charles I, to take the throne. Charles II was given restricted powers, and he accepted the throne on conditions which included adherence to the Magna Carta, Petition of Right, and other statutes that limited the power of the king. Parliament had emerged as the governing body of England and the king could not rule in opposition to its wishes.

The emergence of this democratic ruling philosophy has great significance for law enforcement. Responsibility for making or approving law was taken from the absolute whims of the king, and the function was placed with Parliament. Since people could now influence those laws that governed them, laws would better reflect social or community needs. This is the essence of law and the philosophy we have adopted in the United States.

Charles II's primary direct contribution to law and law enforcement was the passage of the *Habeas Corpus* Act of 1679. This act required law enforcement officials to bring a prisoner before a judge and explain why he was being held. If there was, in the opinion of the judge, good reason for keeping the prisoner in custody, the judge was required to establish a trial date. If, on the other hand, good reason was not given, the prisoner would be released.

Although the entire importance of habeas corpus may not have been recognized then, it still is an important part of judicial processes in the United States. Like many provisions of these early petitions or acts, habeas corpus appears in our own Constitution.

During the reign of Charles II, in response to increasing crime, the Common Council in 1663 introduced a force of paid constables who became known as *charlies*. Because they checked the doors of businesses, they also became known as the *shiver and shake watch*.

46

SOCIAL CHANGE AND CRIME

During this period, along with changes in the processes of lawmaking and implementation, the nature of the social order itself was being completely transformed. Throughout the middle ages England had been predominately rural, and most of its people were either farmers on small tenant farms or were farm laborers. However, the country was becoming urbanized, which created vast social problems. There were many influences at work in creating a new and different society. New lands were being discovered that provided fresh avenues for trade. Technology was advancing, new inventions were being developed, and mass production was coming into existence. In conjunction with this, the demands for goods were ever increasing, and the emerging capitalists were interested in making England more productive.

Enclosures. The changing times and the eagerness of lords to capitalize on the demands for goods were exemplified in the development of *enclosures*. Wool was in demand, and the large landowners began to convert farm land to pasture for the grazing of sheep. Sheep grazing not only required large tracts of land, but at the same time it required little help. As a result, tenant farmers were evicted, and farm laborers were put out of work. Thousands of rural people were without a means of support. In desperate hope of improving their situation, they migrated to the rising urban and industrialized centers.

Urbanization and crime. During the industrial revolution, the displaced rural people as well as other poor people were employed by urban industries, whose owners' only interest was production. They had total disregard for the safety and welfare of employees and exploited them without mercy. Men, women, and children were paid starvation wages, kept at their jobs sixteen hours a day, and worked until they were physical wrecks and unable to continue.

47

When no longer productive, employees were fired and replaced by younger and stronger persons.

Unemployment grew by leaps and bounds, while the rich became richer and the poor became poorer. The squalor and filth of the developing slums were unbelievable and much worse than anything seen since that time. The worst slums or ghettos of today cannot begin to match the conditions then existing in England.

Faced with starvation and with no hope for help, the people obtained money or food in any way possible. The crime rate rose at an alarming pace and was uncontrollable. Youth stole goods to sell to the hundreds of fences (a fence refers to a person or business that buys and sells stolen goods). The fence would actually instruct the children on how to steal and designated goods they could best peddle. This may very well be the real beginning of *juvenile delinquency*. Thousands of women and young girls became prostitutes and roamed the streets in search of customers. Men resorted to every conceivable type of crime, primarily as a means of survival.

The cities, London in particular, were not safe, and men of means dared not walk the streets even during the day. The watch and ward, somewhat successful in the past, was not capable of handling the increased population or crime. Contributing to their ineffectiveness was the rebellion of people against serving on the watch and their practice of employing vagabonds to replace them. These hired substitutes were not only incapable of doing the job, but their actions added even more chaos to the situation. They now had a legitimate reason for being on the streets, which made it easier to steal or pilfer.

Attempts to combat crime. Many schemes were tried in response to the enormous crime problem. Penalties were made severe to the point that practically all crimes were punishable by death. However, the opposite effect was realized since more severe penalties tended to make crime seem more profitable since a greater risk was involved. In addition, a man with a starving family in search of survival did not consider the consequences of being caught.

Rewards were offered for information leading to the apprehension of criminals in an attempt to gain public participation in crime control. This, however, merely encouraged citizens to falsely accuse a neighbor in hopes of gaining the reward. This also encouraged constables to ignore minor violations in hope that success would lead the violator to a more serious offense that would carry a larger reward.

Eventually, many forms of private police came into existence. *Merchant police* were employed by merchants to protect their places of business. *Parish police* consisted of church members serving in rotation to protect members of the congregation. *Dock police* or police employed by shipping companies concerned themselves with protecting goods on the docks. Needless to say, none of these proved capable of handling the problem, and, in fact, their inefficiency and disorganization probably contributed to the problem.

HENRY FIELDING AND BOW STREET RUNNERS

During this period of turmoil and lawlessness, a lawyer-novelist was appointed principal magistrate of Westminster in 1749. Henry Fielding is best known as a novelist, but his contributions to law enforcement are also of great significance. Fielding's concern for lawlessness is typified by his 1750 publication, "An Enquiry into the Causes of the Late Increase of Robberies."[1] This document is an indication of his literary ability as well as a survey relative to the problem of robberies. In fact, Fielding can be credited for having conducted the first actual police survey, which included recommendations for the improvement of law enforcement in London.

As principal magistrate, Fielding took over the police station located on Bow Street and with the help of his blind

---

[1] Douglas G. Brown, *The Rise of Scotland Yard* (New York: G. P. Putnam's Sons, n.d.), p. 27.

49

brother, John, proceeded to establish an improved police force. As part of the improvements, he established what has become the first known detective unit. Men of this unit wore no uniforms and responded quickly to the report of a crime in an attempt to quell the situation or apprehend the criminal. The members of this unit, which became known as *the Bow Street runners*, were entitled to rewards that were offered.[2] The Bow Street runners were not readily accepted by the people, but as they proved themselves successful, the public gradually accepted them and became more and more dependent upon them as law officers.

The runners were disbanded for awhile, but John Fielding, who succeeded his brother as principal magistrate, revived them during his administration. Henry Fielding did not live to see the real success of his efforts, but his brother continued the police reform movement. John's longer administration actually gave him time to make advances beyond the accomplishments of Henry. John developed crime prevention programs such as caring for prostitutes and misguided children, implemented better street lighting on a larger scale, instituted foot patrol, and established horse patrol in order to cover a greater area.[3]

ROBERT PEEL AND THE NEW POLICE

Although many improvements were being made, the real beginning of the modern police system did not take place until 1829 when Sir Robert Peel established a new metropolitan constabulary under the command of a commissioner. Sir Robert Peel was the Home Secretary at the time and the new constabulary derived its existence and authority from a Parliamentary bill which he pushed through to passage.

The significant features of the new metropolitan police were: 1) adherence to semimilitary principles, 2) the quality of the men employed, 3) the discipline that prevailed, and

[2] Douglas G. Brown, p. 28.
[3] Douglas G. Brown, p. 28.

4) the fact that one man was in charge and responsible only to the national government.

Specifically, some of the principles under which the police force was established were:[4]

Know

1. Police officers must be under strict discipline to ensure the necessary high standard of behavior.
2. The absence of crime is an index of efficiency.
3. The force should be territorially distributed.
4. The force should be divided by hours and shifts.
5. Higher positions should be filled by men from the lower ranks.
6. Police officers should wear a uniform and that a good appearance commands respect.
7. Applicants for the police force should be judged on their own merits.
8. Training of police officers assures greater efficiency.
9. The principle object to be attained is the prevention of crime.
10. A perfect command of temper is an essential quality.

It is interesting that these principles are as applicable today as they were in 1829. This portrays the farsightedness of Peel as well as his genius in police reform. It also illustrates the weakness in many of our present day American police departments and their failure to learn from history. Some police administrators have yet to recognize the value of these principles developed over 140 years ago.

The headquarters for the new police force was a small side street called Scotland Yard, thus the origination of the name attached to the London police and their famous address.

The constables for the new police force were drawn from the retired military ranks, thus insuring good discipline and a willingness to don the police uniform. The constables wore top hats and blue coats and were armed with nightsticks. They

[4] Douglas G. Brown, pp. 82–86.

Original Scotland Yard building

By kind permission of the Commissioner of
Police of the Metropolis, New Scotland Yard,
Broadway, London, W.W.I., England

carried no firearms, and this custom still prevails in England
today.

At first, the citizens were contemptuous of the constables and were apprehensive of their authority. This is easily
understood since the people were generally distrustful of the
military and saw Peel's force as a tool for government control. In other words, the citizens were fearful of martial law.
However, as the police proved their effectiveness, the people
not only accepted them but placed them in a position of high
esteem and respect.

In respect for Sir Robert Peel, the constables became
known as *peelers* or *bobbies*. The term bobbies is still used in
England to identify their police officers or constables.

The first Peelers

By kind permission of the Commissioner of
Police of the Metropolis, New Scotland Yard,
Broadway, London, W.W.I., England

DEVELOPMENT OF LAW ENFORCEMENT IN THE UNITED STATES

THE ENGLISH COLONIAL PERIOD

The beginnings of American law enforcement can be traced
to the period of English colonization. Early law and governmental structure were dictated by the king's charters, under
which the colonies were established and ruled. These charters formally confirmed English tradition already customary
to the English settlers in America.

The charters of both the London and Plymouth companies reflected England's philosophy of government and law
enforcement. There was some provision for home rule, but

53

always with national control. The colonists were allowed to administer local matters but only as long as they did not conflict with English law or beliefs. In other words, all governmental activities were subject to the approval of the king and were held within the confines of English tradition and legality.

The London Charter of 1606 typified such control. It stipulated that each colony was to be governed by a resident council appointed from among the residents of the colony. Although this reflected local control, national authority was maintained by having members of the resident council appointed by a superior council whose members were appointed by the king. In terms of local control, the resident council was authorized to: 1) establish ordinances that did not conflict with English law, 2) act as a court, 3) appoint colonial officials such as law and judicial officers, and 4) administer the government of the colony.[5]

Control changed hands frequently as the colonists progressively demanded more control over their affairs. Slowly, after much struggle, democratic self-government became a reality. The emerging country had to pass through much turmoil which included indian wars, the Revolutionary War and the events leading to it, the Declaration of Independence, and, finally, the ratification of the Constitution of the United States.

Southern law enforcement. The agricultural nature of the South practically dictated the type of government and law enforcement to be established. The South's relatively flat, sparsely populated land with its fertile soil and favorable climate made it natural farm country. The people attracted to the South were largely the farming class from the rural areas of England. As they settled, they naturally adopted the county form of government because of their familiarity with

---

[5] John Spencer Bassett, *A Short History of the United States* (New York: The Macmillan Company, 1939), p. 46.

it and because the county unit lended itself to the sparsely populated rural area.

As in rural England, the office of sheriff was established as the primary law enforcement official. The county court was established, and this court originally made the ordinances, directed the sheriff in enforcing them, and handled all judicial matters. Although the county court had great influence, the sheriff was without a doubt one of the most, if not the most, influential and important man in the county. He had full police powers and exercised his authority throughout the county.

Northern Law Enforcement. Although counties were established in New England, the primary government unit was the town. New England was as opposite the South as opposites can be. The North's soil and climate were not as favorable for farming, and because of the fear of Indian attacks, the people settled close together forming clusters of populated areas. It naturally followed that the town became the primary governmental unit. As the problem of Indian attacks subsided, the inhabitants began to move to outlying districts, but by habit they clustered in groups, thereby establishing new towns.

In conjunction with their form of government and urban English background, the colonists established the office of town constable or watchman. As the towns grew larger, the town officials established the watch and ward, patterned after the English system.

As this country grew in both population and area, the North became more dependent upon the office of county sheriff, while at the same time the growing southern cities had to utilize the town constable and watch and ward system. However, even today the office of sheriff in the South practices broader law enforcement functions than his counterpart in the North. Again, the role of the southern sheriff indicates the tradition that was established in rural England and reinforced during colonial times.

Far western and southwestern law enforcement. Although migration to the far west and southwestern United States took place after considerable settlement of the Atlantic regions, mention should be made of Western law enforcement. Actually, the West had characteristics of both the North and the South. The area was vast, but much of it was good for ranching rather than farming. This rural character lended itself to the utilization of the county sheriff and, in fact, this office emerged as the most important.

At the same time, however, the western pioneers had to originally settle in groups in order to protect themselves from the Indians. Therefore, the town also emerged as an important governmental unit and the town marshall became an important law enforcement official.

To encourage the development of both officers was the fact that northerners as well as southerners were moving to the West and bringing with them the tradition of their areas. Those people settling in towns demanded the town constable or marshall, and those settling in the more rural regions demanded the sheriff.

By virtue of the predominately rural character of the West, the sheriff emerged as the primary law enforcement official. Even today, the Western and Southwestern sheriff and his deputies practice full police powers and provide law enforcement services throughout their respective counties. In fact, the sheriff and his deputies may be the only significant law officers serving large areas within their county.

FURTHER DEVELOPMENT OF MUNICIPAL POLICE

As stated previously, the first American police officers were parish constables appointed during the colonial period. Originally, the town probably appointed one constable and added others as the population increased. The first constables were most concerned with the hours of darkness, and night watches were eventually established to patrol the streets. With the continued population growth, night patrol proved quite inadequate, and some cities established a separate day watch.

Wyatt Earp, well-known early Western law enforcement official

U.S. Signal Corps Photo number 111-SC-94117
in the National Archives

Growth of cities. Since the United States was primarily rural, forces developed rather slowly. Not until the late 1700's and early 1800's were there any cities of significant size. In fact, in 1760, Boston and Philadelphia were the largest cities, each with a population of approximately 20,000. New York was the third largest with a population of about 10,000, and Charleston came next with 9,000.[6]

In the 1800's population growth surged significantly, due to both a high birth rate and mass immigration. The

[6] John Spencer Bassett, p. 142.

growth of manufacturing and the resulting need for labor encouraged immigration. Hardships of life in Europe, as well, caused many to leave for a land of greater opportunities. Immigration records show that from 1820 to 1860 over five million aliens immigrated to the United States.[7]

Conflict in the growing cities. Most of the immigrants were laborers for whom the South—with its tradition of slave labor—held little opportunity for settlements. Generally, the immigrants moved to the northern cities, took what employment was available, and resided in areas that were within their financial means. This migration created many social problems, some of which caused a substantial increase in crime and the concurrent need for more and better law enforcement.

Conflicts that frequently resulted in riots arose between the immigrants, especially between the Irish and native-born Americans. Actually, an organization called "Native Americans" was formed which expanded to incorporate chapters within many cities. A riot occurred in Boston in 1837 as a result of conflict between the Irish and the "natives." In 1884, a prolonged riot occurred in Philadelphia as a result of the Catholics' opposition to using the Protestant Bible in the public schools.[8] Of significance is the resemblance these riots have to race riots involving black suppression that occurred during the 1960's.

As industrialization increased, the cities became larger and more complex, thus causing even greater problems for law enforcement. At the time of the Civil War, the country's labor force was quickly changing from one of an agricultural nature to one of an industrial nature. These industrial laborers began to organize into unions for purposes of negotiation with factory owners. Since employee demands were not always granted, mass strikes and sometimes riots resulted.

[7] John Spencer Bassett, p. 461.
[8] John Spencer Bassett, p. 462.

In 1886, the Knights of Labor union called for a strike by railroad employees because a fired foreman was not reinstated. This strike became quite violent with the result that federal troops were called in to quell it. Special constables were not able to control it. Buildings were burned, and innocent people were killed during mob violence. In the same year a labor riot occurred in Chicago with the result that seven police officers were killed and sixty were injured. Of course, there were mass arrests and considerable property damage.[9]

Patterns of development. As stated previously, the rural character of the United States up to the present century inhibited the growth of municipal police departments. As the cities grew, however, they had a greater need for protection and an increasing demand for not only a larger police force but also for a more effective one.

The pattern of development of the police department in most cities was from military protection or martial law to the appointment of a single watchman, to a constable or marshall, to a night watch, to a separate day watch, to the combination of both the day and night watch which was eventually subdivided into wards, and finally to the establishment of a formal police department under the direction of a chief of police or commissioner. Such development was not usually smooth but rather was haphazard and confusing. More often than not the organization, supervision, and control of the law enforcement agency shifted frequently. For example, many police departments would first be under the control of the mayor, and later under the control of the commissioner. Similar shifts back and forth can be found in many other areas as well.

The first actual night watch was established by Boston in 1636 followed by New York's *rattle watch* in 1658 and Philadephia's night watch in 1700. New York's rattle watch

9 John Spencer Bassett, pp. 741–742.

was so called because the watchmen used rattles to announce their presence and to communicate with each other. The slow growth of cities and, consequently, police departments was evidenced by the lapse of over one hundred years before there was a need for night watches in cities such as Cincinnati and New Orleans. Cincinnati established its night watch in 1803 and New Orleans in 1804.

As in England, the early night watches were anything but effective. They had the appearance of vigilantes and were often lazy. Usually, members of the watch were citizens who had to rotate the responsibility among themselves. Like their counterparts in England, these citizens frequently hired substitutes who often were less than respectable citizens. It was also not uncommon for a court to sentence a minor misdemeanor to be a watchman as a form of punishment.

Daytime policing did not come into existence until 1833 when the city of Philadelphia established a day watch, followed by Boston in 1838, Cincinnati in 1842, and New York in 1844. As the first, Philadelphia had twenty-four day watchmen and one hundred twenty night watchmen who were all under the command of a captain. Later, Philadelphia went back to a separate night watch, and in 1854 the then existing force was directed by a marshall who was elected for a two-year term. A few years later, the office of marshall was abolished, and the police agency came under the direction of a chief of police who was appointed by the mayor.

Following the successful pattern set in England fifteen years earlier by Sir Robert Peel, New York, in 1844, became the first city in the western hemisphere to establish a modern police department. New York, by adopting Peelian principles years before other cities, proved itself to be one of the most energetic American cities in terms of law enforcement. In fact, there are still cities today that may be further behind times than Peel was in 1829.

Other cities, to mention a few, that followed New York with the establishment of formal police agencies included Chicago in 1851, Cincinnati in 1852, Philadelphia in 1855, Baltimore in 1857, and Detroit in 1865.

American police agencies were slow also in comparison to London's bobbies in adopting official police uniforms. Unfortunately, the early watchmen, constables, and police officers saw the uniform as a symbol of degradation and refused to wear it. In fact, when New York first suggested uniforms, the police officers protested vigorously and actually refused to wear them. Finally, in 1856, twelve years after the establishment of the department, New York police adopted a full police uniform and became the first such uniformed officers in the country. Even then, however, the problem of identification was not fully solved, as each ward of the city was allowed to adopt a uniform of their choosing.

Although Henry Fielding established the Bow Street runners around 1750, it was more than one hundred years later before American police agencies recognized the need for and significance of a detective unit; it was not until 1866 that Detroit established a detective bureau as one of the early ones in the United States. New York established a detective bureau in 1882, and Cincinnati established one in 1886.

The primary method of patrol in the early days was by foot, and it was not until the late 1800's that horses were used to any great extent. Generally, the cities were rather concentrated, but as they began to spread over a larger area, mounted patrol became a necessity. In 1873 Detroit established one of the earliest mounted units to patrol the city's outskirts. Philadelphia began its mounted patrol in 1889 with the purchase of ninety-three horses.

The use of horses as the chief means of patrol was relatively short-lived. With advent of the automobile, police on foot or horseback found themselves unable to apprehend motorized law violators. Philadelphia began using motorcycles in 1906, and Detroit modernized with the installation of their motorcycle patrol in 1909. In that same year, Detroit's police commissioner, at his own expense, purchased an automobile for patrol. The Commissioner was reimbursed, however, after the automobile proved itself, and, in fact, other autos were added to the force shortly afterwards.

61

Other municipal police developments during the early twentieth century included the adoption of the telephone, the use of radio-equipped police cars, the installation of teletype systems, the use of fingerprint systems, and the employment of policewomen, etc. These and many more advances were occurring at an accelerated pace. Cities were growing rapidly and by necessity were becoming more dedicated to providing efficient law enforcement services. The conflicts of the times such as race riots, labor riots, and general rise in crime forced additional developments in law enforcement.

Horse-drawn police wagon in Philadelphia in the late 1880's

Courtesy of the Philadelphia, Pa.
Police Department

Officer Walter Stick, May 1921, with the first radio-equipped patrol car in the United States

Courtesy of the Detroit, Mich. Police Department

THE STATE POLICE

In comparison with municipal police, state police agencies are of relatively recent origin. As the United States con—tinued to grow and expand, the need for law enforcement services also grew. In many instances, the existing municipal agencies could not adequately handle crime, since criminals were not confining their activities within the municipality but were operating throughout the state. Corruption and political patronage also existed in some police agencies to the extent that the broader governmental unit had to develop a more centralized arm of the law. All things combined, crime was continually increasing, and there was a definite need for the state to become directly involved in providing law enforcement services.

Although corruption and inefficiency at the local levels of law enforcement were sometimes factors in the development of state police, another influential factor was that the state did not have an agency to enforce rules and regulations deemed necessary by it. Instead, the state had to rely completely upon the municipal or county law enforcement officials to carry out the state's sanctions. If a particular law was unpopular, the sheriff and other officials were likely to ignore its enforcement rather than cause unrest among constituents. The local law enforcement officer identified much more closely with his local situation and had little concern for the desires of state government.

State police forerunners. The first agency similar to our present day state police was the Texas rangers. This force was established by the Texas provisional government in 1835 when Texas was still a republic. It was actually a military unit under the direction of military authorities. The act of 1835 established three ranger companies with the primary responsibility of border patrol. One of the major border problems concerned the rustling of Texas cattle by Mexicans who took the cattle back to Mexico; consequently, the apprehension of rustlers became one of the rangers' primary tasks. They also investigated crimes within the state, and today the Texas rangers have confined themselves primarily to investigations and to assisting other law enforcement agencies within the state.

Massachusetts was the next state to recognize the need for a state-wide enforcement agency. The appointment of a small force of state officers or constables in 1865 was in direct response to the need to control vice within the state. The constables were also given general police powers, and, therefore, Massachusetts can rightfully claim the establishment of the first law enforcement agency with general police authority throughout the state. This unit did not last long as such and was replaced in 1879 by a state investigation unit called

Texas Rangers, Company G, at Alice, Texas, in 1903

Courtesy of the Texas Department of Public Safety

the district police which was later incorporated in the state police established in 1920.

After a lapse of thirty-eight years following the establishment of the Massachusetts state constables, Connecticut established (1903) a state detective force patterned after the Massachusetts district police. This force also was primarily concerned with vice control, such as gambling and enforcement of liquor laws. The force was also too small and unstable to accomplish much and was finally absorbed into a more effective organizational unit.

Next to be established were the Arizona rangers in 1901 and the New Mexico mounted police in 1905. Like the Texas rangers, they were more or less a border patrol rather than a

The Arizona Rangers, 1901–1909

Courtesy of the Arizona Department of Library and Archives
Phoenix, Ariz.

state police agency. Their fate, however, was not as good as the Texas rangers, and they both eventually ceased to exist.

Emergence of the state police. The first modern state police agency was the Pennsylvania constabulary, established in 1905. The ill-conceived state police agencies established prior to 1905 were created in response to limited needs, such as frontier problems or the enforcement of usually unpopular vice laws.

The Pennsylvania constabulary, on the other hand, originated to serve multiple needs: 1) to provide the governor an executive arm to assist him in accomplishing his responsibilities, 2) to have a means of quelling the riots that were occurring during labor disputes in the coal regions, and 3) to improve law enforcement services in the rural portions of the state where county officials had been less than successful.

The first reason is clearly illustrated in Governor Pennypacker's statement relative to the establishment of the agency:

In the year 1903, when I assumed the office of chief executive of the state, I found myself thereby invested with supreme executive authority. I found that no power existed to interfere with me in my duty to enforce the laws of the state, and that by the same token, no conditions could release me from my duty so to do. I then looked about me to see what instruments I possessed wherewith to accomplish this bounden obligation—what instruments on whose loyalty and obedience I could truly rely. I perceived three such instruments—my private secretary, a very small man; my woman stenographer; and the janitor, . . . So I made the state police.[10]

The second reason, to quell riots and disorders, resulted from labor disputes primarily between coal miners and the mine administrators. The local sheriffs and constables were unable to cope with such massive disorder, making a larger and more centralized police agency essential.

The third reason is somewhat typical of the times and again illustrates the then existing problems related to local law enforcement. The primary characteristic that set Pennsylvania off from its earlier counterparts was the concept of rural law enforcement and its organization. From its inception the Pennsylvania state police was under the administrative control of a superintendent appointed by the Governor. It was a uniformed mounted force that operated from an arrangement of troops and troop substations situated throughout the state so that protection was afforded in even the most remote areas. This force was well organized and served as a blueprint for other states to follow. With the establishment of the Pennsylvania state police, modern state policing had emerged.

FEDERAL LAW ENFORCEMENT

Federal law enforcement agencies, like the state police, emerged as a result of the many problems faced by a fast growing country. The fantastic increase in population, urban growth, the rise of industrialization, technological advances,

[10] Katherine Mayo, *Justice to All: The Story of the Pennsylvania State Police* (New York: G. P. Putnam's Sons, 1917), pp. 5–6.

Pennsylvania State Troopers on strike duty in Chester, Pennsylvania, in April 1908

Courtesy of the Pennsylvania State Police

and the broadening of the country by ratification of new states all contributed to the need for controlling legislation that could only be enforced by the centralized government. For example, the advent of the automobile made it possible for criminals to commit a crime in one jurisdiction or state and be in another within a relatively short time. Advances in communication allowed the planning of a crime in one jurisdiction with its perpetration in another. In addition, communications media also aided specific crimes such as gambling and fraud. Local police, ununited as they were, found it virtually impossible to prevent such crimes or apprehend criminals from within the confines of their bailiwick.

Actually, the Constitution of the United States, by virtue of its many provisions, made it imperative that investigative and enforcement agencies be established at the federal level. Although the Constitution did not specifically establish law enforcement agencies, Congress does have the implied power by virtue of Article I, Section 8 (see Chapter 1) authorizing them to enforce or carry into effect provisions of the Constitution and its amendments. For example, the Constitution provides authority to lay and collect taxes (Article XVI) and, therefore, Congress has the authority to establish the Internal Revenue Service as an enforcement agency. The Constitution stipulates that Congress has power to coin money and punish counterfeiters (Article I, Section 8) and, concurrently, Congress also has the authority to establish an agency to detect and arrest counterfeiters. Without such agencies to enforce laws of such magnitude to the entire country, counterfeiting would run rampant, and there would be no means to effectively collect taxes.

Unlike the states, who required a police force with broad general powers, federal law enforcement agencies resulted from the passage of specific laws, and, therefore, they had somewhat limited functions. Federal agencies did not come into existence in an orderly manner, but instead they developed haphazardly as a result of the passage of controlling legislation. This does not mean, however, that enforcement agencies were established concurrent with legislation. In fact, enforcement agencies usually were established several years after the legislation went into effect and only then when the law was proven ineffective without enforcement.

Actually, Congress purposely avoided the establishment of such centralized law enforcement agencies. The Constitution reserved police power or authority to the states, and the consensus of opinion was that this right should not be infringed upon. In addition, citizens generally were in fear of a federal police force as this suggested a "police state." Therefore, the development of federal law enforcement agencies was slow; agencies were usually not established until mass violations made them absolutely imperative.

The forerunners. The forerunner of federal law enforcement was the office of United States marshall, established by Congress in 1789. As the first federal law enforcers, marshalls were appointed to federal districts throughout the United States. In this capacity they functioned as the only existing enforcement arm of the United States government. It was not until 1861 that Congress placed the marshall under the administrative control of the attorney general along with United States district attorneys. The early years of the marshalls were quite colorful, as they were often assigned to the frontier areas of the country. Today their functions are primarily connected with judicial processes. Generally speaking, United States marshalls have responsibilities similar to those of sheriffs, but they are concerned with federal rather than local law.

Also, in 1789, in reaction to the growing problem of smuggling, Congress inaugurated a Revenue Cutter Service. Following this, Congress did not establish additional law enforcement agencies for forty years. Finally, the government became concerned with mail robberies and frauds. The Postal Act was passed, authorizing postal agents to enforce the Act's provisions. Enforcement of postal laws was again strengthened in 1836 when Congress authorized the postmaster general to pay agents for investigating postal matters.

In 1842, the counterfeiting act was passed, and three years later the secret service was organized to enforce its provisions. Between the years 1882 and 1886, the problems of immigration and smuggling led to the establishment of the U. S. border patrol within the customs service. In 1906, the pure food and drug regulations were established to combat the unhealthful ways that foods were being processed within many factories. This regulation, of course, necessitated special agents for enforcement. This pattern of passing legislation and then establishing enforcement agencies persisted throughout the years until a multitude of federal agencies were in existence. The one agency that added great impetus

70

to the development of federal law enforcement was the secret service, and it deserves additional mention at this time.

Three U. S. Marshals of the San Antonio, Texas District in the early 1880's: "The Kid," Tom O. Bailes, and Sam Walker

U.S. Signal Corps Photo number 111-SC-93366
in the National Archives

71

Secret service. During the Civil War, counterfeiting became so prevalent that Congress was forced to recognize the need for a law enforcement branch of the Treasury Department. The counterfeiting law was passed in 1842, but of interest is the fact that the secret service was not established until 1865. This agency's primary responsibility was to restore faith in United States currency by detecting and arresting counterfeiters.

The secret service proved to be exceptionally effective, but they were certainly not without their problems. Originally, the agents carried as identification only a written letter of appointment which did little to dispel the suspicions of citizens and businessmen who questioned the agents' authority and who were reluctant to cooperate in investigations. This identification problem continued for approximately eight years until in 1873, the Treasury Department issued all agents printed credentials and a badge.

The main significance of the secret service is that it was the first general investigative agency of the federal government. In fact, for years it was the primary law enforcement agency of the United States, and other federal departments frequently borrowed secret service agents to conduct investigations for them.

Federal Bureau of Investigation. The best known of the federal law enforcement agencies is the Federal Bureau of Investigation. The history of the FBI is quite colorful and reveals a great deal relative to the times. It specifically illustrates the legislature's reluctance to organize a central police agency.

Although the office of Attorney General was established in 1789, it was not until 1870 that the Department of Justice was created with the attorney general as the chief administrator. The creation of the Justice Department is attributed to the post-Civil War reconstruction problems and the need for the centralization of legal activities at the federal level. By this action, the attorney general assumed the tasks of prosecuting federal violators, formerly handled separately by the various governmental departments. During the early years of the department, the attorney general had only one "special agent" to conduct investigations. For most of such work, he expected his attorneys and marshalls to act as investigators in addition to their other responsibilities. He also hired detectives for specific investigations or borrowed secret service agents. Actually, this practice of borrowing secret service agents was followed by many other departments. Congress would authorize money for the borrowing of secret service agents, but it would not authorize money for Justice investigators.

Finally, after much effort by the Justice Department and much resistance from Congress, Attorney General Bonaparte was given sufficient appropriations that allowed him to establish a permanent force of detectives within his department. Bonaparte acted swiftly by having able secret service agents who had worked for him from time to time transferred to his department. This force worked relatively well, but as the department grew, unsound practices crept into the emerging organization. Finally, in 1924 the FBI was organized and placed under the able leadership of J. Edgar Hoover, who had been an employee of the department since 1917. Under his leadership, the FBI quickly became the most efficient and respected law enforcement agency in the United States.

Summary

Archaeological findings give evidence that some form of law enforcement existed even during ancient times. Such law enforcement was, of course, based primarily on the need for protection against marauders or for the enforcement of elementary social codes. As society became more complex, so did the type and degree of enforcement policies and principles.

Generally speaking, law enforcement developed concurrently with the development of law. The first known codification of laws was that of Hammurabi, ancient king of Babylon. This legal code was concerned with such matters as responsibilities of the individual to the group and private dealings between individuals. The existence of law naturally required the existence of a mechanism for enforcement. As law developed, the mechanism became continually more elaborate.

Law enforcement developed rather slowly during ancient and medieval history, but many events during that time influenced the emergence of law enforcement as we know it today. To appreciate and understand current law enforcement, it is imperative that one be familiar with the contributions of such people as Pisistratus, Solon, Augustus, and the English kings during medieval history.

A very critical need for effective law enforcement came into existence in London when, as a result of the industrial revolution, the city became urbanized. In response to the concurrent crime problem, Sir Robert Peel created the first modern police organization: the new metropolitan constabulary. This new police agency became the model for those that were eventually established in the United States.

Law enforcement in America developed in a rather haphazard manner, with the Southern colonies adopting the English sheriffs system, and the North their constable or town system. Municipal police systems evolved further with

the growth of cities. As the cities grew, the demand for
police services multiplied. In the United States, police
departments in most cities developed from military protection,
or martial law, to the appointment of a single watchmen,
to a constable or marshall, to a night watch, to a separate
day watch, to the combination of both the day and night
watch, and finally to the establishment of a formal police
department.

State police agencies came into existence for a variety
of reasons, such as the inability of municipal agencies to
handle mobilized interstate crime activities and corruption
in some local agencies. Others were created to meet the need
for an executive arm to enforce state laws. Federal law
enforcement agencies, like the state police, emerged as a result
of the many problems faced by a fast growing country.

Discussion Questions

1. Discuss the relationship between the development of law and the development of law enforcement agencies.
2. Discuss the early Greek and Roman contributions to the development of law enforcement.
3. Discuss the Anglo-Saxon contributions to the development of law enforcement.
4. Discuss the governmental structure of Anglo-Saxon England and its influence on law enforcement.
5. What were the contributions of King William toward the development of law enforcement?
6. What is Henry I famous for relative to law enforcement?
7. What was the Court of Star Chamber?
8. What effect did the Industrial Revolution have on law enforcement?
9. Discuss the development of municipal law enforcement in the United States.
10. Discuss the development of state and federal law enforcement agencies in the United States.

3

State of the Art

Police agencies in the United States—with its rapid and erratic growth—developed in a rapid, haphazard, and sometimes contradictory manner. This statement is not necessarily critical of the police, but rather is critical of local government wherein the police have developed.

By tradition, law enforcement is a local matter, and, therefore, the development of the police naturally reflects the quality of local government. Police efficiency, quality, image, and prestige are clearly dependent upon the quality of local government and reflect the attitudes of those representatives administering government.

Early police departments, like local governments, were often inefficient and incompetent. Most, if not all, early police departments were traditionally impregnated with political appointees who were often corrupt and who were not necessarily concerned with individual rights. Even today, there are departments so ingrained with such traditionalism that appointments and promotions are still politically made. In many cities such patronage exists throughout the ranks, and a complete reorganization occurs with the election of succeeding mayors. However, even though such problems still exist to some extent, the police have advanced considerably and are now knocking at the door of professionalization.

LAW ENFORCEMENT AS A PROFESSION

Recognized professions include such fields as law, medicine, theology, and education. Can the police service join their ranks and also be considered a "true" profession? This question has been debated for several years, and debate will undoubtedly continue for several more. Actually, however, those who claim a professional status for the police service are being unrealistically optimistic.

There has been much said about what is required for professional status, and there is ample literature that lists the criteria or characteristics of a profession. However, these lists often have little in common and are often contradictory. It would seem, therefore, that professional status is a broad term which means different things to different people.

Police officers are eager for professional recognition, and they have devised numerous supporting rationales. In supporting their claim they often point to such things as amount of recruit or in-service training, efficiency, appearance, and an elaborate organizational structure. These are all elements or criteria for professionalization, but by themselves they do not justify the claim.

Unfortunately, much of the effort toward achieving professionalism has been directed toward the total organization rather than the individuals within it. Certainly, administrative concepts and organizational designs are important, but more important are the individuals working within that framework. Before the police service can be considered a profession, each and every person involved must be a professional. Each police officer must be totally dedicated, possess a healthy attitude, be interested in self-improvement, and have a firm grasp of that field of knowledge peculiar to law enforcement.

Perhaps a reasonable approach is to identify the common characteristics of the identifiable professions and then determine if law enforcement possesses these elements. If law enforcement does, perhaps it can lay claim to professional status. If it does not, then it may not justifiably make the claim.

In comparing the accepted professions, those characteristics that seem to be common to all are: 1) ample professional literature, 2) research, 3) the existence of and participation in professional organizations, 4) an ethical code of conduct sworn to by all, 5) a devotion by all members toward self-improvement, and 6) the existence of an identifiable academic field of knowledge peculiar to that profession in conjunction with a formulized educational prerequisite.

By these standards, it becomes immediately clear that law enforcement as a total is *not* a "true" profession. However, the situation is not as bleak as many would believe. In recent years, great strides have been made, and it it clear that success eventually will be realized.

Progress, although slow, has accelerated recently as a result of societal demands. The police have had to struggle to merely keep pace with technological advances .and social change.

As will be recalled, law enforcement is a blanket term that includes enforcement at the federal, state, and local level. The various law enforcement agencies are striving toward professionalization at varying rates. Generally speaking, federal law enforcement agencies better reflect professionalism than do most local agencies. This is not to imply that federal law enforcement is alone in such an accomplishment, nor is it to say they have actually reached the "true" professional level. State and local police agencies have also, in varying degrees, advanced toward the goal. Some are within reach, some have exceeded federal agencies, and some have lagged behind.

The greatest encouragement can be derived from the fact that the police are involved in all the criteria believed necessary for professionalization. They have not sufficiently progressed in any one of the areas, but progress is constant in all areas. The federal government should be credited with providing the necessary impetus for the improvement in local and state law enforcement agencies.

FEDERAL INFLUENCE

In recognition of the nation's crime problem and the need for improving law enforcement, the federal government initiated several programs to study the problem and to assist local law enforcement. This participation by federal government initiated a surge forward toward professionalization. Federal interest was best typified by the creation, in 1965, of a Commission on Law Enforcement and Administration of Justice, the passage of the Law Enforcement Assistance Act of 1965, and the passage of the *Omnibus Crime Control and Safe*

Streets Act of 1968. These programs were of such significance and influenced the professional criteria so greatly that they need to be discussed fully as a prelude to the present involvement of law enforcement in the professional criteria.

ρεπd

Commission on law enforcement and administration of justice. This commission was established on July 23, 1965, in recognition of the urgency of the nation's crime problem at that time. The Commission was instructed to inquire into the causes of crime and delinquency and to issue recommendations for preventing crime and delinquency and improving law enforcement and the administration of criminal justice.

The work of the Commission was initially divided into four major areas: 1) police, 2) courts, 3) corrections, 4) assessment of the crime problem. As the Commission's work proceeded, special task forces were formed to study organized crime, juvenile delinquency, narcotics, and drunkenness. Finally, a task force in science and technology was also organized.

The Commission's research and inquiries took many forms and included broad-scale surveys, analysis of data available from federal law enforcement agencies. and conferences. Advice was sought at every step from experts in law enforcement, criminal justice, and crime prevention. Finally, the results of the Commission were published in ten documents, each covering a task force subject.

The mere formation of the Commission created nationwide interest that directed attention to the criminal justice system. Police were looking critically at their own department. The public became painfully aware of police problems and the apparent ineffectiveness of the criminal justice system. Legislatures began reviewing laws with an intention of improving them, and many states established similar commissions. All in all, everyone became more aware of the law enforcement problems and more concerned with solutions.

The published task force reports were a hallmark in police literature. They attacked the issues, discussed without reservation the failure of criminal justice, and offered recommendations for improvement. The reports provided guidelines for improvement. Criminal justice leaders pored over the reports and implemented many changes which did improve criminal justice.

A primary value of the Commission and the resulting reports was that the issue of criminal justice was forced upon legislatures and local politicians. No longer could they avoid the issue. It was before them, demanding subsequent action.

Law Enforcement Assistance Act. The Law Enforcement Assistance Act of 1965 also resulted from the federal government's concern with the problem of crime. This act which created the Office of Law Enforcement Assistance (OLEA) was signed by the President on September 22, 1965. The act made funds available to states, localities, and private organizations to improve methods of law enforcement, court administration, and prison operation. Briefly, the act authorized federal grants to public or nonprofit agencies to improve training of personnel, to advance the capabilities of law enforcement bodies, and to assist in the prevention and control of crime. The Law Enforcement Assistance Act also authorized the United States Attorney General to conduct studies, render technical assistance, evaluate the effectiveness of programs undertaken, and disseminate information on the projects.

Under this act, which concluded June 19, 1968, federal support was given to 359 separate projects. The projects included training, research, demonstration efforts to prevent and control crime or to improve criminal justice agencies, and the giving of assistance in upgrading personnel. Four hundred twenty-six grants and contracts were given, totaling 20.6 million dollars, to grantees or contractors in all fifty states, thus causing national influence on criminal justice.

The act was the first federal law giving money to local government for improvement of law enforcement. The accomplishments under it were quite significant to law enforcement. For example, during the act's duration, 2.5 million dollars were allocated for general recruit and in-service training, and .8 million dollars for higher education. Like the Commission on Law Enforcement and Administration of Justice, this act and resulting activities were without precedence and added great impetus to the achievement of professional law enforcement. OLEA was also influential in that moneys from it supported much of the work done by the Commission. In reality, the two were partners to some extent, and their concurrent roles strengthened each other. The Commission identified weaknesses in criminal justice to which OLEA could direct its attention and OLEA provided financial assistance to the important work of the Commission.

Omnibus Crime Control and Safe Streets Act. This act, commonly referred to as the *Safe Streets Act* became effective on June 19, 1968. The Safe Streets Act repealed the Law Enforcement Act of 1965 but was committed to fulfilling the existing obligations of OLEA. The new act established the Law Enforcement Assistance Administration (LEAA) which was responsible for carrying out the provisions of the bill.

The Safe Streets Act was a milestone for the nation and addressed itself to some of the most urgent problems in criminal justice. It offered federal funds to help states and local communities plan, coordinate, and attack the crime problem. The origins of this bill can be found in the studies conducted by the previous President's Commission on Law Enforcement and Administration of Justice, some of which was funded by OLEA. The Safe Streets Bill incorporated recommendations made by the Commission and reflected the experiences of OLEA.

Title I of the Safe Streets Bill provided funds for planning and initiating action programs to strengthen law enforcement. More specifically, it provided funds for 1) the creation of state planning agencies, 2) action grants to improve and strengthen all aspects of criminal justice, 3) academic assistance grants to encourage higher education, and 4) the establishment of a National Institute to conduct research relative to crime prevention.

The Safe Streets Bill provided impetus for the creation of state planning agencies and subsequent state comprehensive law enforcement plans. It also provided funds, channeled through the state agency, which improved police operations throughout the United States. The bill also caused many law enforcement personnel to seek additional education by providing grants and loans for such purposes. In addition, the act allowed pre-service students of law enforcement to obtain loans which were excused when they became employed by a law enforcement agency.

The Safe Streets Bill was obviously the culmination of all federal programs for local law enforcement and has had, by far, the greatest impact. As a result of such federal interest, law enforcement has improved, is continuing to improve, and such improvement moves law enforcement toward becoming a profession. *stop*

PROFESSIONAL LITERATURE

For years there was a definite lack of good professional literature in the fields of police administration, police technology, and law enforcement in general. Books were the exception rather than the rule, and the number of law enforcement periodicals were few.

In recent years publishers have become increasingly interested in publishing books and periodicals in the police field. Probably the most influential factor in increasing the availability of professional literature has been the growing number of college-level law enforcement programs. Not only have these programs created the need for textbooks, but also they have provided police educators with an opportunity to publish and share information.

There is still a need for quality professional literature, but that need is gradually being met.

Police officers from various police agencies in library

Courtesy Harrisburg Area Community College
Harrisburg, Pa.

PROFESSIONAL ORGANIZATIONS

Perhaps one of the most influential professional law enforcement organizations is the International Association of Chiefs of Police (IACP) which has a membership exceeding six thousand. The IACP has been very active in upgrading law enforcement across the country, has encouraged cooperation between police agencies, and has disseminated professional information to all police agencies.

The IACP has been particularly active in the areas of developing training standards, developing instructional materials, encouraging education, and providing consulting services on a fee basis to law enforcement agencies. In fact, endorsement by IACP has resulted in the acceptance by po-

86

lice agencies of many modern innovations. The results of this organization's efforts are highly visible throughout the law enforcement field.

Not all law enforcement agencies in the United States are represented in the IACP membership, and in all probability some never will be. However, membership representative of the greatest possible number of agencies is highly desirable in furthering professionalization of law enforcement.

One limitation of the IACP is that active membership is limited to chiefs of police or law enforcement executive officers. It is an organization for management personnel and does not necessarily represent the lower echelon within the law enforcement ranks. This is not to suggest that membership should be open, but illustrates the need for professional organizations for the lower ranks.

Most states have statewide as well as local law enforcement associations. It is common, for example, to find state associations of chiefs of police, training officers, juvenile officers, investigators, and others representing a specific police activity. Most state groups also have highly specialized committees and subcommittees and sponsor annual conferences and professional seminars. Some associations are more active than others, but all are concerned with upgrading police service.

Lambda Alpha Epsilon is another national association that exists for the purpose of upgrading criminal justice. This association's membership is limited to police officers and police aspirants who are enrolled in college law enforcement programs. The association began in California, but as more colleges have adopted law enforcement programs the membership has grown significantly. In recent years Lambda Alpha Epsilon has regionalized its organization and has chapters throughout the United States. The prerequisite for membership is advanced education, and therefore, it would seem the organization can become significantly influential.

Another national organization is the Fraternal Order of Police (FOP) which has chapters throughout the United

States. Membership consists primarily of patrolmen, and hundreds of municipal police departments have their local chapter.

Although considerable activity exists, there are still many directions these associations can take that will provide impetus for better law enforcement. They need, for example, to become more actively involved in training programs, work more closely with colleges and universities, and encourage professional standards for all law enforcement personnel.

RESEARCH

Research is a vital part of all professions, but until recent years little research was conducted in law enforcement. In fact, for years law enforcement existed on pure traditionalism with little emphasis on experimentation or attempting to determine better and more rewarding techniques. Actually, little research was done until 1965 and then it was a result of the critical crime problem throughout the United States. At that time, and also as a result of the crime problem, the Federal Law Enforcement Assistance Act was passed which provided additional impetus for research.

A giant stride in research was made with the passage of the Safe Streets Bill of 1968 which, among other things, established a National Research Center. This center, in Washington, D. C., has conducted a great deal of research which has been quite enlightening to law enforcement nationally.

Much has been done in the research areas, but there is much more to be accomplished.

CODE OF ETHICS

A hallmark of a profession is a code of ethics that is adhered to by all within that profession. There is a Law Enforcement Code of Ethics which very adequately depicts the ideals and common goals of the law enforcement officer. Unfortunately, however, many police officers are unaware of this formalized code. Therefore, they do not realize that the ideals set forth

Four fundamental

1. Civil participation
2. Community rental
3. Oiemanit response
4. countallied

EL PASO COMMUNITY COLLEGE
COLORADO SPRINGS, COLORADO
POL 101 - Introduction to Law Enforcement

COURSE REQUIREMENTS

CLASS TIMES: Tuesdays, 6:00 - 9:00 ~~P.M.~~, Fort Carson 2216

INSTRUCTOR: LTC Fred J. Villella 3427, 2715, 2620

PHONE: 579-3427

TEXT: American Law Enforcement

CLASS MEETINGS:
22 June 1976 Chapter 1
29 June 1976 Chapter 2
6 July 1976 Chapter 3 (First Paper)
13 July 1976 Chapter 4
20 July 1976 Chapter 5 (Midterm) ✓
27 July 1976 Chapter 6
3 August 1976 Chapter 7
10 August 1976 Chapter 8 (Final)

GRADING AND TESTING: Two exams will be given, each is worth 50 points for a
composite possible of 100 points for the quarter

B = 89 to 80

C = 79 to 70

D = 69 to 60

U = 59 and below

W = official withdrawal

PAPERS REQUIRED: ONE typewritten pages answering the question, "I am
interested in Law Enforcement because...". Grading
on this paper will be <u>acceptable</u> or <u>unacceptable</u>. An
acceptable paper constitutes completion required work
and the grade achieved on exams remains as earned. An
unacceptable paper lowers the letter grade earned to the
next lower letter grade. Papers are due by the third
class. Unacceptable papers may be redone until an acceptable level is achieved, up to the day of the final exam,
and as many times as is necessary to reach an acceptable
level.

REQUIRED READING: How to Win Friends and Influence People, by Dale Carnegie.
Three pages minimum, typewritten paper critizing Mr.
Carnegie's book. This paper must justify your thoughts
on how this book might not be of benefit to a law enforcement officer. Any book in the criminal justice field
may be substituted (check with instructor).

Law Enforcement Code of Ethics

As a Law Enforcement Officer, my fundamental duty is to serve mankind; to safeguard lives and property; to protect the innocent against deception, the weak against oppression or intimidation, and the peaceful against violence and disorder; and to respect the Constitutional rights of all men to liberty, equality and justice.

I will keep my private life unsullied as an example to all; maintain courageous calm in the face of danger, scorn, or ridicule; develop self-restraint; and be constantly mindful of the welfare of others. Honest in thought and deed in both my personal and official life, I will be exemplary in obeying the laws of the land and the regulations of my department. Whatever I see or hear of a confidential nature or that is confided to me in my official capacity will be kept ever secret unless revelation is necessary in the performance of my duty.

I will never act officiously or permit personal feelings, prejudices, animosities or friendships to influence my decisions. With no compromise for crime and with relentless prosecution of criminals, I will enforce the law courteously and appropriately without fear or favor, malice or ill will, never employing unnecessary force or violence and never accepting gratuities.

I recognize the badge of my office as a symbol of public faith, and I accept it as a public trust to be held so long as I am true to the ethics of the police service. I will constantly strive to achieve these objectives and ideals, dedicating myself before God to my chosen profession . . . law enforcement.

in the code should be an integral part of their lives. This does not mean that officers do not live by its standards. By virtue of dedication to service most officers do live by the code even though they may be unfamiliar with it.

Regardless of conduct, however, all officers should be familiar with the Law Enforcement Code of Ethics, and let it serve as a framework within which to direct their lives. Devotion to the code is absolutely necessary since it pertains directly to each and every individual. Only professional individuals make a profession.

SELF-IMPROVEMENT

Dedication to self-improvement by every law enforcement officer is imperative before professionalism can be realized. Officers must have inquisitive minds, must question aspects of law enforcement, and must exploit every possible opportunity to improve themselves. This improvement, of course, is usually best achieved by participating in training and education programs. Therefore, it is necessary that law enforcement officers extend themselves to make such opportunities available. Many departments have initiated pre-service and in-service training programs during the last few years, but there is still room for improvement. All departments must become involved with or make available self-improvement programs in such areas as supervision, middle management, management, community relations, and in specialized techniques. Law enforcement will become a profession only after such programs are available and utilized nationwide.

FIELD OF KNOWLEDGE

The recognition of the need for law enforcement educational programs and their subsequent development has been the most encouraging step in the climb toward professionalization and is, perhaps, the key to achievement. Sound educational programs not only reflect their field of knowledge, but as more and more officers attain degrees, their excellence will give strength to the other professional criteria. Such men will, by virtue of their education, be prone to become concerned with and involved in all those activities that reflect a profession. The growth of law enforcement education programs in our colleges and universities can be considered the most significant development in law enforcement since the existence of the police service. In view of such prominence, the law enforcement student should be knowledgeable of the development of this role.

POLICE EDUCATION

The very nature of the police function demonstrates the importance of providing educational opportunities to police officers. The police are charged with safeguarding the lives and property of all citizens, the prevention and suppression of crime and delinquency, and protection of individual rights. Such vast responsibilities definitely demand all police officers be intellectually aware of their responsibilities and possess the ability to perform accurately and efficiently.

In performing their duties the police must be able to act without hesitation and very often make instantaneous and legal decisions that would take a court months to reach. Individual constitutional rights of all citizens are also realized through the actions of the police, and, in effect, people realize their rights through the interpretive actions of the police. To a large degree, therefore, our democratic way of life is dependent on the ability and effectiveness of the police in upholding and administering the laws of the land.

In the present era of sociological change, scientific development, and technological advance, the field of police service has widened tremendously. For example, with the rapid growth of urbanization, police responsibility has proportionately increased. Each year police take on more and more responsibility which greatly increases the complexity of their task.

91

Police officers attending a college-level class in police adminis-tration

Courtesy Harrisburg Area Community College
Harrisburg, Pa.

Another major factor which demands police education is the increased need for effective administrative techniques that are necessary to cope with the increasing size of police agencies. In fact, many of our present police departments are comparable in complexity to our largest business enterprises which demand highly effective and creative administrative ability.

In view of the need for police education, it is believed that the colleges of this country, if they are to serve the educational needs of the community, have the responsibility for providing law enforcement programs. In fact, if the police service is to maintain merely its present level of efficiency, the colleges must provide such educational opportunities. Each year a higher percentage of high school graduates go on to college. Normally, in the absence of a police curriculum, students will prepare themselves educationally for employment in other areas. If police programs are not established, the source of supply of qualified police officers will increasingly shrink in terms of highly qualified individuals; it can be assumed that the shrinking source of supply of police officers will consist largely of those who lack the ability or the initiative to attend college.

RESISTANCE TO POLICE EDUCATION

Resistance to police education is weakening in most parts of the country as more and more chiefs are practically demanding that programs for their officers be established. In fact, most of the law enforcement programs that have come into existence during the past few years are a result of their efforts.

Perhaps the only real remaining obstacle to program development is some lack of mutual understanding on the part of the police chief and the college administrator. The educators and law enforcement officials must meet as equals for discussion and must erase any misconceptions or suspicions that may exist. The police need to realize that the college is a service institution with no other interests beyond that. The college administrators must recognize and appreciate the practical needs of law enforcement and must attempt to establish programs that meet these needs.

IMPETUS FOR POLICE EDUCATION

Although we can trace police education back to 1907 when the University of California at Berkeley established a program for law enforcement officers, the actual impetus for the development of police education did not really occur until a much later date. In 1963, the Ford Foundation provided a grant to the International Association of Chiefs of Police for the purpose of improving standards for police education. As a result of this grant and the work in conjunction with it, many community colleges and universities throughout the country established law enforcement programs. Prior to

IACP's work there were fewer than one hundred such programs, most of which were in California. By the end of the four-year grant period there were over two hundred such programs throughout the United States.

The next boost to police education occurred with the passage of the Law Enforcement Assistance Act of 1965. Among other things, OLEA offered financial aid to several colleges so that they could establish programs in law enforcement. Generally, the grants were given to colleges in states where no such programs existed. With the establishment of these programs, other colleges were encouraged to embark upon similar programs. The recent rapid growth of police programs can be largely attributed to the influence of the Ford Foundation grant to the IACP and to the establishment of the Office of Law Enforcement Assistance.

Another boost was provided by the passage of the Omnibus Crime Control and Safe Streets Act of 1968. This act covered many areas of concern to law enforcement throughout the United States, but of importance to education was the appropriation of funds to assist police officers and police aspirants in achieving a law enforcement education. The bill provided loans and grants to police officers and police aspirants enrolled in law enforcement programs. It further authorized the total cancellation of any such loans at the rate of 25 percent for each complete year of law enforcement service after graduation. Quite obviously, this bill encouraged hundreds of police officers to pursue college-level work.

It is expected that the trend toward higher education will continue, and will continue to exert an influence in all areas necessary for police professionalization.

PHILOSOPHY OF LAW ENFORCEMENT

As in all academic or professional areas, the evaluation of a law enforcement education philosophy has not been smooth and without controversy. Also, as in all professions, such differences of opinion will continue to exist.

In reviewing the development of police education, it appears that three distinct philosophies exist. For purposes of clarification, they can be identified as vocational, humanistic, and professional.

Vocational. The curriculum established within the framework of the vocational philosophy has an emphasis on the tools, skills, and techniques of police work. In essence, the primary thrust is to train men how to do their job. In conjunction with this emphasis, the curriculum is geared very closely to the local situation and may include skill-oriented courses such as radio dispatching, firearms training, defensive techniques, pursuit driving, state vehicle code, state criminal code, and first aid. The individual completing such a curriculum is in a position to don a police uniform and go directly into the field. Such a curriculum often replaces the need for the police academy and may, therefore, be very beneficial to those departments that may not possess the resources necessary for such training.

Humanistic. A program within the humanistic philosophy is usually typified by a pure liberal arts education with emphasis on the social or behavioral sciences or is based on a sociology curriculum. This philosophy indicates that the law enforcement task or function is such that there is no need or justification for more specific courses in law enforcement.

The curriculum may, however, have a strong correctional emphasis and may concern itself with the relationship between the police function and the activities of correctional agencies such as parole, probation, or penology. Examples of humanistic programs are often difficult to illustrate, since they are often not identified as such and may be identified synonymously with "liberal arts."

Professional. The professional philosophy seems to be the most prominent and probably has had the greatest impact on law enforcement. This philosophy recognizes that there is a field of knowledge intrinsic to law enforcement in which the police officer should be conversant and knowledgeable. The curriculum, like the humanistic approach, is also concerned with behavioral sciences, but recognizes a value in their immediate relationship to law enforcement.

The professional curriculum should provide a broad intellectual and professional background that will help the officer better utilize communicative skills in writing reports and expressing thoughts, to more efficiently and effectively accomplish his task, to be conversant with the structure of government and its philosophies, to understand and appreciate the managerial functions of police departments, and to be well grounded in psychology, criminology, and human relations in order to understand the ramifications of the problems which confront him daily.

The professional courses or those specifically related to law enforcement are also of an academic nature and are designed to expand the student's knowledge of the actual implementation of psychological and sociological concepts. In essence, the professional philosophy includes the offering of professional courses taught in conjunction with the liberal arts, communicative arts, and behavioral sciences. This philosophy recognizes the existence of a definite field of knowledge peculiar to the law enforcement service and includes such knowledge along with general education. Such professional courses are not technique or skill oriented, but are of a broad academic nature. The curriculum is constructed to develop the student's intellect and also to improve his professional competence, which will ultimately help him to more efficiently fulfill his responsibilities as a law enforcement officer.

The objectives of such a philosophy might include:

1. Development of competencies that will enable students to gain employment with the various law enforcement agencies.
2. Development of leadership qualities that will help the student to progress through the higher positions in his agency.

3. The fostering of ideals of professional achievement in the police service.
4. The provision of a broad intellectual framework within which the student can direct his efforts, both personally and professionally, in a more intelligent and meaningful manner.

LAW ENFORCEMENT:
AN EDUCATIONAL DISCIPLINE

The foregoing discussion on police education provides the necessary background information necessary to determine whether law enforcement is an *academic discipline* or a *professional discipline*. However, before discussing law enforcement and its adaptability as an academic discipline we must first define the words *academic* and *discipline*. *Webster's New Collegiate Dictionary* defines *academic* as "pertaining or belonging to an academy, college, or university, or to colleges." A second listed definition is "literary, classical, or liberal rather than technical or professional." *Discipline* defined by *Webster* in the instructional or educational sense is a "branch of knowledge involving research" and "training which corrects, molds, strengthens, or perfects."

Combined, the definition of an academic discipline would be "literary, classical, or liberal education combined with research and offered at the college or university level." It would seem that this definition in its present form would exclude law enforcement from the ranks of the traditional academic family. In its strictest sense, the definition requires constant involvement in research and excludes those subject areas that are professionally or technically oriented. Law enforcement is becoming more and more involved in research, but most of the research is conducted by social scientists rather than law enforcement academicians. Certainly, most law enforcement educational programs have a professional or technical orientation. Because of these orientations, law enforcement cannot be considered an academic discipline in the strictest interpretation of what an academic discipline is.

In the strictest sense, law enforcement education must be considered as a professional discipline rather than as an academic discipline. This, however, is not a dilemma since there are many other prestigious professional fields under the same heading. By this definition in the academic world, law enforcement is placed side by side with law, medicine, engineering, and education. They, like law enforcement, cannot be called academic disciplines because they are professionally or technically orientated rather than being of a classical or literary nature. Educationally speaking, law enforcement is a professional discipline rather than an academic discipline and is a respected and accepted college or university level program.

If one were interested, however, a good case could be presented to claim law enforcement as an academic discipline. Degrees issued by colleges and universities reflect the nature of study pursued and, in effect, the degree identifies the "academic discipline" from that of the "professional discipline." Good's *Dictionary of Education* defines a degree as "a title bestowed by a college or university as official recognition for the completion of a course of study or for a certain attainment." The same source defines an *academic* degree as "(1) a degree offered for attainment in liberal education, (2) more broadly, a degree conferred by an institution of higher education, regardless of the field of study." It is in the second and broader sense that the term is most commonly used today, and, therefore, almost all degrees are generally thought of as *academic*.

As in the case of academic degrees, the academic disciplines are also thought of in broader terms. This broader and commonly accepted definition would include law enforcement and the other "professional disciplines" which involve some technical or professional education.

It should be restated, however, that technically speaking law enforcement is a "professional discipline" rather than an "academic discipline." There is no stigma to such a classification and law enforcement officers should stand proud of such professional education and their professional degrees.

TECHNOLOGY AND LAW ENFORCEMENT

Technology has played an important role in law enforcement for some time, but recent years have seen greater emphasis in this area. Technological improvements have been made especially in the areas of computerization of records, communications, transportation, weaponry, criminal investigation, and crime detection. The greatest improvement has been in the area of the application of science to crime detection, but in recent years there has been an increased interest in other areas as well.

Some important possibilities that were reported by a federal task force include:

1. Electronic computers for processing the enormous quantities of needed data.
2. Police radio networks connecting officers and neighboring departments.
3. Inexpensive, light, two-way portable radios for every patrolman.
4. Computers for processing fingerprints.
5. Instruments for identifying criminals by their voices, photographs, hair, blood, body chemistry, etc.
6. Devices for automatic and continuing reporting for all police car locations.
7. Helicopters for airborne police patrol.
8. Inexpensive, reliable burglar and robbery alarms.
9. Nonlethal weapons to subdue dangerous criminals without inflicting permanent harm.
10. Perimeter surveillance devices for prisons.
11. Automatic transcription devices for courtroom testimony.

Modern police equipment

Courtesy of the Cleveland, Ohio Police Department

All of these devices are not "of the future" since many are already in operation and others are being developed. In addition, as law enforcement turns to technology, there is no question that other innovations not presently envisioned will come into existence.

All of these, of course, are in addition to those devices already in general use among most police agencies. For example, there are many instruments that can measure the blood-alcohol content of a person in determining whether he can be prosecuted for drunk driving. The lie detector is in general use in most police agencies and has aided in hun-

Administration of lie detector examination

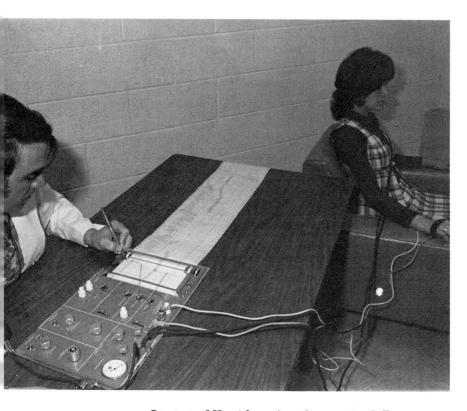

Courtesy of Harrisburg Area Community College
Harrisburg, Pa.

dreds of criminal investigations. The lie detector has also been widely used in selection of personnel as well.

Computers are being used in our large departments, and they can retrieve information on stolen vehicles or wanted persons within seconds. These computers can also predict crime incidence by area, which allows a more efficient assignment of personnel.

In the laboratory, many kinds of analyses are made in conjunction to criminal investigations. A narcotic can be identified within minutes. A fiber can be identified as coming from a person's clothing. Dust from the cuff of a suspect's

101

pants can be compared with dust at the scene. Bullets can be matched with a certain gun, etc. The crime laboratory plays an important role in crime detection and this role will undoubtedly continue to broaden throughout the future.

Summary

Police agencies in the United States developed in a rather haphazard manner and were often inefficient. Many agencies were staffed with political appointees and were corrupt. Even today we find police departments so ingrained in traditionalism that appointments and promotions are still politically made.

There is much controversy over whether or not law enforcement has reached a professional status. Generally, law enforcement is involved in all the characteristics that are common to accepted professions, but not to the extent to justify a professional status. Great strides are being made, however, and professional status is within reach.

The need for college-educated police officers is becoming more obvious every year. The importance and diversity of the police function demands that police officers be better prepared to assume their tasks. Police education generally is new on the national scene, but there are now over three hundred colleges with law enforcement programs.

It appears that three district philosophies of law enforcement exist: 1) vocational, 2) humanistic, and 3) professional. The vocational approach stresses skills and techniques and relates to training rather than education. The humanistic approach can generally be equated to a liberal arts education. The professional approach stresses a field of knowledge that is intrinsic to law enforcement.

Many technological improvements have been introduced to law enforcement in recent years. These improvements have been most obvious in the areas of computerization of records, communications, transportation, weaponry, criminal investigation, and crime detection.

1. Is law enforcement a profession? Discuss.
2. What influence has the federal government had on local police during the past few years?
3. What is the importance of police education?
4. What has been the primary impetus for police education during the last decade?
5. Differentiate between the three philosophies of police education.
6. Is law enforcement an academic or professional discipline?
7. How will technological advances affect the police service?
8. What were some of the problems of early law enforcement agencies?
9. What is the relationship between the police department and the city it serves?
10. What is the status of research in law enforcement?

4

The Police Function

The municipal, county, and state police of the United States are charged with responsibilities which rank second to none in importance in our democratic society. The police service is that branch of government that is assigned the awesome task of securing compliance to the multitude of laws and regulations deemed beneficial to society. Since law is society's means of achieving conformance to desired norms, the police are society's agents for the maintenance of harmony within the community. Within this broad context, the police are charged with the safeguarding of lives and property, the prevention and repression of crime, the prevention of delinquency, and the protection of individual rights.

The police have not always had these broad responsibilities. For years the police, and even the public, generally believed the police were fulfilling their full responsibility by investigating crime and attempting to apprehend criminals. There was little thought given to the concept of prevention, and most certainly citizens did not expect the police to intervene in domestic disputes or problems related to their youngsters. The problem of raising youth was a family responsibility and was kept within the family.

In our rural past, conformity to the social norm was achieved through *folk-policing*. That is, people refrained from certain activities for fear of being admonished by neighbors. In our present mobile and urbanized society *folk-policing* is minimized, and the public depends upon the police to fill the gap. The fear of admonishment no longer prevails and, therefore, people are less restrained from deviating from society's demands.

Although the police function is old, it has, of necessity, changed to meet changing needs. The process of law enforcement has gone through a gradual development along with the country's urbanization which has enlarged the police role significantly.

The police resisted change, but the forces of time were unrelenting, and their role widened to meet the new needs of each new generation. Even today the police resist change, but they are becoming more and more open-minded, and as a result are able to more readily assume additional and different responsibilities.

The police of this country have very admirably met the challenge of changing times, but there are certain societal expectations beyond their capability. For example, even under the most favorable conditions the police cannot eliminate crime. The police do not create the social conditions conducive to crime nor can they resolve them. The police do not enact the legislation that they must enforce. They do not adjudicate the offenders they arrest, and they are only one of the agencies of criminal justice.

In order to appreciate what the police do to achieve the complex objectives of law enforcement, it is necessary to review the "line" functions or methods which directly attack the problems.

PATROL

Patrol refers to the moving on foot or by vehicle around and within an assigned area for the purpose of obtaining information relative to serving the police function. Officers are usually in uniform, and when a vehicle is used, it is usually conspicuously marked. The marked vehicle is often referred to as a "uniformed unit" since, like an officer's uniform, the markings identify it as a police car.

The purpose of patrol is to distribute police officers in a manner that will eliminate or reduce the opportunity for citizen misconduct and to increase the probability of apprehension if a criminal commits a crime. These are the two primary concerns of the potential criminal, and where effective patrol minimizes his chances of success, he will refrain from committing the crime.

The patrol function is the backbone of police operations and has the broad basic responsibility of public protection and service. The patrol force is on twenty-four hour surveillance and should be able to respond quickly to all situations requiring police attention. The most important police operation is patrol, and its effectiveness will determine the success of the entire police agency.

The patrol function is so basic to fulfilling the police responsibility that its goals are essentially synonymous with the total police objective. These objectives include the prevention and suppression of crime, the safeguarding of lives and property, the apprehension of criminals, the control of traffic and noncriminal conduct, and the provision of public services. In achieving these objectives, the patrol force checks buildings, surveys possible incidents, questions suspicious persons, gathers information, regulates traffic, enforces traffic regulations, responds to reports of crime, conducts preliminary investigations, and arrests violators of the law.

Before discussing fully the activities involved in the achievement of patrol objectives, the organization of patrol must be made clear.

GEOGRAPHICAL DISTRIBUTION OF PATROL

In order to be effective, the patrol force must be geographically distributed so that response time to crime incidents is minimized. Vehicles and men must be assigned to definite geographical areas that will assist them in the achievement of the patrol responsibility. Such geographical breakdowns are referred to as beat, sector, and precinct.

Beat. The fundamental unit of patrol is the beat. The beat is that area within which patrol officers are assigned either on foot or within a marked unit. The officer assigned to a beat is responsible for all activities within the area and must provide continuous surveillance throughout his tour of duty. All calls originating within his beat are referred to him and he makes the original contact.

Since the beat is the fundamental unit of police patrol and, in fact, the entire police organization, it is important

109

that it be constructed properly. Unfortunately, many police departments arbitrarily design beats without regard to the needs to be met.

Beats cannot be constructed solely on the amount of ground to be covered and the number of people in the area, but on a combination of many factors. If properly designed, the beat will vary in size and shape according to such factors as population density, the type of area, the crime problem, topography, past called-for services, and geographical characteristics. An ill-conceived beat will not only disproportionately distribute the workload, but will also contribute to the ability of criminals to commit violations.

The manner of determining beats is not always given the attention it deserves. Quite frequently the same beats are used throughout the twenty-four hour day and year after year. Not only do changes in need occur from year to year, but the needs may very well be different throughout the day. Beat arrangements demand constant evaluation and should be changed as conditions change.

Sector. A patrol sector consists of several beats and is so divided to facilitate proper supervision. The patrol supervisor usually holds the rank of sergeant and is often referred to as the "line supervisor." His task is to coordinate activities of the several beats and to assist patrol officers when needed. One of his major tasks is to instruct beat officers or correct patrol techniques and to subsequently see that such techniques are practiced. For general purposes, therefore, the sector is a division for supervision.

Precinct. Larger cities have so many beats and sectors that it becomes necessary to have another larger division. The precinct relates to a large district which is comprised of several patrol sectors. Like the sector, the precinct is a geographical division that facilitates coordination of the activities of the smaller geographical units. Usually, the only justification for a precinct is an area too large to be handled by smaller divisions. Like beats, the precinct should be so located that it facilitates the accomplishment of the police objective.

THE PATROL OFFICER

The patrol officer is not only the most important police position in the police department, but it is the most challenging. The patrol officer is responsible for all activities within his beat and must patrol continuously throughout his tour of duty. He must practice proven patrol techniques, be alert to all situations, and respond to all calls within his area. This means he will become involved in activities ranging from looking for lost children or writing a traffic summons to conducting the preliminary investigation of a murder. He has the greatest responsibilities of all police positions, and he must be able to cope intelligently with them.

His importance is obvious when it is realized that he is at the implementation level of the police function. The best-conceived plans of executive officers are entirely dependent upon the patrol officer's ability to put them into practice. In addition, the patrol officer is at the grassroots level and is the one in direct contact with society's problems. He makes the physical arrest, he stops the traffic violator, and he prevents crime.

Many departments throughout the United States have adopted the "generalist" theory which places the major emphasis of police service on the patrol officer. The generalist theory minimizes the specialist and requires the patrol officer to accomplish as much of the police task as possible. The generalist patrols the streets, issues traffic violation notices, investigates accidents, and conducts preliminary investigations of all crimes within his beat. In fact, where feasible, the generalist will investigate a crime to its conclusion with the resulting arrest of the offender. In most cases, the generalist conducts the entire crime scene investigation so that the detective merely picks it up at that point and carries it onward.

PATROL DISTRIBUTION BY TIME

Another important factor in patrol is the distribution of man-power according to the time of day. Like the determination of beats, many police departments have arbitrarily divided the patrol officers into three "platoons" with each working on one of three "shifts." A platoon refers to the group of men working a particular shift and shift refers to a division of the day.

In determining shifts, the police must consider such criteria as the times of called-for services and the workload over certain blocks of time. The shift change should occur when there are the fewest calls and when police activity is at a minimum. The shift hours should, as nearly as possible, equalize the workload on each shift.

During shift changes, police availability is significantly reduced, and the opportunities for criminal activity are increased. Traditionally, police departments have thought in terms of three shifts which has necessitated almost total inactivity by police during certain hours. To illustrate, assume the shift changes at twelve midnight. Since police vehicles are usually used around the clock, the officers on the previous shift will need to start to headquarters prior to midnight. For example, they may leave their beat at approximately 11:40 PM. Those officers going on duty will pick up the car at midnight, but it may take them until 12:20 AM to reach their assigned beat. Therefore, the police have been absent from that beat for forty minutes.

This problem has existed for years, but police departments have finally begun to rectify it. One solution is to have overlapping shifts. This merely entails dividing each platoon in half with one group coming in an hour earlier than usual and the other half coming in an hour later than usual. The following illustrates this arrangement:

OVERLAPPING SHIFTS

Normal shift hours *All officers*	Overlapping shifts	
	1st platoon	*2nd platoon*
8 AM–4 PM	7 AM– 3 PM	9 AM–5 PM
4 PM–12 midnight	3 PM–11 PM	5 PM–1 AM
12 midnight–8 AM	11 PM– 7 AM	1 AM–9 AM

Another method has been to add a fourth shift which may overlap two other shifts. For example, if the traditional 8:00 AM–4:00 PM, 4:00 PM–12 midnight, 12 midnight–8:00 AM were used, the fourth shift may work 6:00 PM–2:00 AM or some other overlapping combination.

Another method of patrol distribution by time that is working well is the *ten–four* (10–4) plan. This plan replaces the traditional eight-hour shift with a four-day week of ten hours each day. This system permits a shift overlap potential of six hours and an increase in the number of patrol beats. More important, the *ten–four* plan permits the department to deploy manpower so it is greatest during the busy hours. Another advantage may be the possible increase in morale due to three days off each week.

Following is an example of a time schedule utilizing the *ten–four* plan. It must be remembered, however, that each department must tailor its time schedule to meet its specific needs.

TEN–FOUR SHIFT SCHEDULE

Shift	Hours
I	7 AM–5 PM
II	4 PM–2 AM
III	9 PM–7 AM

It will be noted that this time schedule provides extra manpower and patrol coverage during the hours of 4:00 PM to 5:00 PM and 9:00 PM to 2:00 AM. The assumption with this time schedule is that the overlapping hours represent the time of greatest workload.

The number of men on each platoon must also be given serious consideration. It is virtually impossible to equalize the workload on each shift and at the same time have low activity shift change times. Invariably, one eight-hour period will vary in workload from another. Traditionally, police departments have mistakenly divided the men into thirds with one-third assigned to each shift. Frequently, this means that one platoon has a greater or lesser workload than another, even though the manpower is the same. Obviously, this should be avoided, and the number of men assigned should be in accordance with the workload of each platoon.

TYPES OF PATROL

The two basic types of patrol are walking and the well-marked automobile. The foot beat is the oldest form of patrol, but the advent of the automobile has made foot patrol less useful. There are still some cities in the United States utilizing foot patrolmen, but generally, most police departments have abandoned this practice in favor of motorized patrol.

As a result of the automobile, the population has become less concentrated and has spread over a larger area. It is, therefore, virtually impossible for the police to patrol on foot the vast area within which the people live.

Additionally, of course, the automobile itself became a police problem that could only be solved with the use of police cars. If police officers were on foot, the motorized public could generally drive as they pleased with little chance of a policeman catching them.

Generally speaking, in a motorized age it is impossible to police the mobile public while on foot. The police must be motorized in order to adequately fulfill the police responsibility.

This is not to say that foot patrol cannot be used effectively. In highly populated business areas a foot officer may be very effective. There may be areas, for example, where a car cannot patrol because of heavy traffic or because of narrow alleys and walkways between buildings. Foot patrol is also useful to regain citizen support simply by personal contact, since motorized patrol has taken much of the human perception of the police officer away from the public. However, before using foot patrol officers, the police department should be sure that a more effective means of patrol is not available. Generally, foot patrol is only justified in a highly populated business district where there is pedestrian and vehicle congestion as well as an abundance of crime. Of interest is the fact that many police departments are motorizing their foot patrol officers by putting them on motor scooters. This decreases response time and also allows more coverage by each officer.

Mounted Texas Rangers on manhunt, supported by modern communications equipment and Department of Public Safety helicopter

Courtesy of the Texas Department of Public Safety, Austin

Other types of patrol include the use of horses, motorcycles, aircraft, and boats. In many instances a combination of two or more of these patrol methods, in conjunction with modern communications equipment, are required to meet

115

specific needs. For example, the police may utilize horses, jeeps, walking men, and a helicopter when searching for lost hunters or a lost child. They may use the patrol car in conjunction with directions from observers in a helicopter when searching for a criminal suspect or chasing a fleeing felon.

Many cities have large harbors or waterways within their jurisdiction and, therefore, utilize boats. In such cases they have highly trained officers commanding the boats who are engaged in activities ranging from enforcing boating regulations to investigating smuggling activities. They usu-

Patrol boat of the Detroit Police Harbormaster Division

Courtesy of the Detroit Police Department
Detroit, Mich.

ally work quite closely with the United States Coast Guard as well as pursuing their own responsibilities.

The helicopter is probably the most recent development in police patrol. During the last few years many police organizations have adopted helicopters. State police organizations and highway patrols use the helicopter for traffic control and for emergency medical treatment at accident scenes. The helicopter is also very useful when searching large areas and for transporting emergency medical supplies to hospitals. Municipal police agencies use the helicopter quite effectively in patrol since they can observe rather large areas with

Air medical evacuation helicopter used for transporting victims of accidents

Courtesy of the Arizona Department of Public Safety

117

clear visibility. They can, for example, direct a ground patrol car when chasing escaping felons. These are just a few examples of the use of the helicopter, as it can be adapted to many policing situations very effectively.

PATROL AND CRIME PREVENTION

The primary means by which patrol prevents crime is through being conspicuous and available. The obvious presence of the police discourages the criminal from committing a crime for fear of being caught. This indicates the importance of the conspicuously marked vehicle. Not only does this show their presence, but it also gives the impression of police saturation.

The appearance of police saturation is a result of the noticeability of the police unit. Every time it passes, the citizenry will see it, whereas a less conspicuous car would be observed less frequently. The public identifies the car rather than the driver and, therefore, assumes a different car has passed each time, when it is actually the same vehicle. In other words, the citizen thinks he has seen fifteen different police cars, rather than having seen the same car fifteen times.

The uniform car also tends to gain voluntary compliance to the law from motorists. The sight of the police unit causes them to be more observant of traffic laws. Of importance too is the fact that the uniform car is observable from great distances and over a wide area. Therefore, its presence will affect many people at the same time. The more conspicuous the police unit, the more people it will affect at any given time.

Patrol officers can prevent crime by becoming familiar with juveniles within their patrol area or beat. A healthy relationship built on mutual respect between the patrol officers and juveniles will do more toward the prevention of delinquency than any other police activity. The patrol officer is the man the juveniles see and identify as the authority

118

symbol. Respect for the officer promotes respect for the law, and such respect will discourage aggression.

A very important role of patrol in crime prevention is the securing of information that can be passed to other units of the police department. With such information the specialized units can work on a potential problem prior to its actually becoming a problem. The patrol officer is on the street and is in the best possible position to gain information on such things as the formation of a juvenile gang, the underlying frustrations of the community, the use of narcotics, etc. By virtue of his closeness to the community, the patrol officer must keep alert to anything and everything that might indicate a potential problem.

APPREHENSION OF CRIMINALS

When prevention fails, apprehension during or immediately after commission of the crime becomes the next objective of patrol. Alertness on the part of patrol officers leads to the apprehension of a large number of criminals who are: 1) about to commit a crime, 2) committing a crime, or 3) escaping after the commission of a crime. In fact, the large proportion of police arrests are made by patrol officers.

The ability to make these apprehensions is directly related to proper beat layout and chronological distribution of the patrol force. In other words, to increase the potential for making arrests the patrol areas must be designed as a result of an analysis of called-for services, crime patterns, and crime frequency. This coupled with continuous patrol will allow the observant officer to make apprehensions before and during the commission of a crime.

Directly related to apprehension is quick response to calls. Generally, patrol should be able to respond to all calls within a maximum of five minutes and much quicker to calls of "crime in process." Frequently, businesses that are prone to robbery or burglary will have an alarm system which notifies the police upon the initiation of a crime. Certainly, with proper response time the police can often arrive before the perpetrators have left the scene. Of course, like everything else related to patrol, adequate response time is dependent upon proper beat determination.

To facilitate the capture of criminals after the commission of a crime, it is often necessary to have formalized tactical response plans. Tactical plans include standard operating procedures relative to the proper approaches and precautions to be utilized when responding to certain calls. Examples of this are the nonuse of sirens when answering a prowler call, and approaching a building from corners in order to cover all four sides.

More formalized tactical plans are those that are specific to certain offenses or to certain locations. For example, the police should identify potential robbery victims such as banks and develop a plan to be initiated if a robbery occurs. This might entail the assigning of quadrants surrounding the scene, the establishment of roadblocks to seal off the area, and the coverage of probable escape routes. Such preconceived plans will allow quick implementation, which will enhance the probability of success in apprehension.

Unfortunately, many police departments do not have such formalized plans, and this often allows the offender to escape. In fact, the lack of tactical plans may very well contribute to criminality and the probability of escape because of the lack of coordination.

REGULATION OF TRAFFIC AND NONCRIMINAL CONDUCT

The traffic role of patrol is quite obvious and is the most familiar to the public. Traffic control includes the direction of traffic; traffic enforcement through the use of verbal and written warnings; the issuance of citations; and the investigation of traffic accidents. The traffic task is very demanding, and a great deal of police time is devoted to it.

There are police administrators who would like to disclaim the traffic responsibility on the basis that the police job should be crime control rather than traffic control. They believe another city department should assume the traffic responsibility, thus allowing the police to devote full attention to crime prevention and control.

There are many reasons why this is not feasible. If the police accept their primary responsibility of safeguarding lives and property, they must accept the traffic responsibility. Since traffic accidents are a major "killer" in our modern society and since property damage is a result of traffic accidents, traffic control must be accepted as a police responsibility.

It must also be remembered that motor vehicles are used in most crimes. The automobile is used to go to and from the crime scene, it is used to transport stolen property, and auto theft itself is a crime. Because of such use, it is impossible to divorce crime from traffic and traffic from crime.

Additional support for the police handling of traffic control is the large number of criminal arrests resulting from traffic activities. Frequently, a vehicle is stopped for a minor infraction, but when the driver is checked, it is found he is wanted by the police. Quite frequently, also, the police find stolen goods or contraband within violators' vehicles.

Traffic involvement by the police also will help prevent crime. Constant traffic surveillance and frequent stopping of cars may very well discourage the would-be burglar from committing an offense. He may be on the way to commit a crime, but if stopped by the officer, he will realize a better chance of police identification if he commits the crime in that area.

Involvement in traffic will also aid the officer in becoming familiar with people on his beat. Although he may not always be stopping cars, he will as a result of his traffic role pay more attention to all vehicles and, therefore, be somewhat familiar with cars common to his area. A strange car may quickly come to his attention.

A very important benefit from traffic involvement is the frequent opportunity for contact with the public. The police

Highway patrol officer assisting the injured at an accident scene

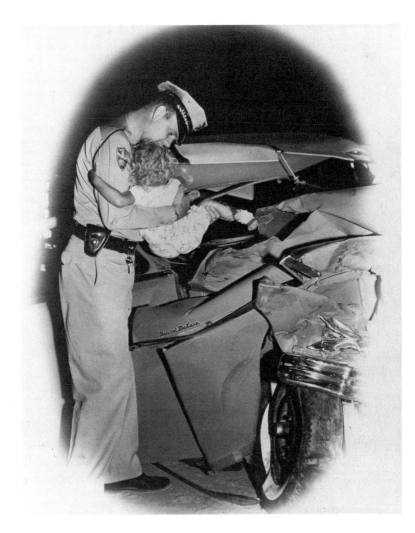

Courtesy of the Arizona Department of Public Safety

come in contact with the public more often in pursuing traffic activity than in any other police function. This is their greatest opportunity to demonstrate efficiency and to create a good image. Of course, the violator dislikes being stopped, but the employment of proper tact even in this type of contact will do much toward creating an image of professionalism.

PROVISION OF SERVICES

One role of the police is the provision of services ranging from giving directions to answering questions relative to points of interest. This role is inescapable due to the twenty-four hour availability of the police and their easy identification as a representative of that jurisdiction.

Rendering assistance is perhaps one of the best opportunities to improve or maintain the police image. Seemingly little problems are of great importance to the troubled person, and understanding help in time of stress is greatly appreciated. The police should give particular attention to rendering assistance, and they should do it with courtesy and demonstrate real concern for each person's problem. The police should realize that a visitor's impression of a city is often synonymous with his impression of the police.

There are those who believe the police should direct their total efforts toward the important activities of crime prevention and crime suppression. However, the provision of services provides the police their best opportunity for achieving many of the crime preventative activities with which they are involved. Provision of services would include such things as providing information, directions, advice, general assistance, and special services.

Information can refer to the routine duties of providing motorists directions and finding locations within a municipality, or it can refer to the more sophisticated reports of crime data and other statistics with which the police are involved. The police are also in a unique position to provide assistance in the form of advice to other governmental agencies as well as private agencies within the community. For example, the police, by virtue of their presence in the field, are in a unique position to detect deficiencies in control devices and report such deficiencies to the traffic engineering or maintenance division of the city. In addition, they are in a position to detect hazardous conditions which may exist within the public realm of the city as well as with private agencies who seek such cooperation.

General assistance, of course, refers to any and all activities which are provided as a courtesy by the police department. General assistance should not infer special privileges to members of the community, but merely refers to services that can justifiably be related to safety in the community.

PATROL EFFICIENCY

The foregoing very aptly demonstrates the importance of the police patrol function. Actually, by virtue of the broad involvement, if patrol were 100 percent successful, there would be no need for specialized activities such as criminal investigation, traffic, or crime prevention bureaus. In fact, the degree of specialization in a police department is dependent upon the success of the patrol function. The police only need to specialize to the extent that patrol is unsuccessful. If patrol prevents all crime, there is no need for detectives, jails, photography specialists, juvenile officers, etc.

Of course, it is virtually impossible for patrol to be 100 percent successful. Even if there were policemen on every block, there are certain crimes that would be committed. For example, murder is often a family affair, in that most are committed within the family unit. Additionally, a large number of murders and assaults are "lovers' quarrels" which are usually within the confines of private homes.

In any event, because of its importance, it is imperative that patrol operate as efficiently as possible in order to minimize other needs within the department. Personnel for specialized units comes from the patrol force, and it is, therefore, necessary that such depletion be carried out with caution. Before strengthening specialized units, for example investigation, the administrator must be assured that the patrol operation cannot be improved to lessen the need for additional detectives. In addition, caution must be exercised in such reassignment, since patrol efficiency may be reduced to a greater extent than what is achieved by the added detective strength. For example, the detective workload may justify another detective for forty hours weekly. The addition of the forty hours in investigation commensurately reduces the man-hours of patrol. Perhaps this loss to patrol reduces efficiency to the extent that forty more hours are needed in investigation to offset the loss.

The important thing is not to weaken the patrol strength unjustifiably in order to strengthen other specialized units. The patrol force is the backbone of the police agency, and its strength should be depleted only when adequate justification exists.

CRIME PREVENTION

Traditionally, the police role has been the apprehension of law violators, but the prevention of crimes has also become generally recognized as an equally necessary and important police function. In fact, apprehension of law violators automatically prevents crime by deterring many who might believe that the opportunity to successfully commit a crime does exist. There has been some resistance to the police crime prevention role, and even today there are a few who believe the police should not concern themselves with formalized crime prevention activities. These people, however, fail to recognize that the traditional activities of police have not been entirely successful. Crime has increased tremendously in recent years. Realizing that traditional methods have not been entirely successful, the police must, of necessity, look to other supporting methods to better reach their goals.

It should be realized that attention to the crime prevention role of law enforcement is not entirely a new concept. In his book published in 1920, Fosdick devoted a full chapter to crime prevention. He said, "All police work has as its goal the prevention of crime." Fosdick also pointed out: "There is as much room for crime prevention in our communities as for fire prevention or the prevention of disease, and in this endeavor to limit the opportunities of crime and keep it from claiming its victims the police department must take a leading part."[1]

Unfortunately, the police field has been slow in accepting such responsibilities. Like all social institutions, the police have resisted change and have maintained the traditional view which imposes few administrative problems. Such agencies must recognize their broader responsibilities and assume an active role in crime prevention.

In reality, although they may fail to recognize it as such, the police have always been involved in an elementary role of crime prevention. The attention to apprehension may very well discourage others from committing crime for fear of their own apprehension. The presence of police, whether organized or not, tends to discourage potential violators. Of course, these activities are not sufficient in themselves, and more formulized action is imperative.

Earlier we discussed the role of patrol in crime prevention. This role cannot and should not be minimized since crime prevention can best occur at that level. There is, however, the need for other crime prevention activities that supplement the patrol function. These activities include working with juveniles, improving community relations, becoming involved in community organizations, educating the public, and cooperating with other public service agencies.

JUVENILE UNIT

Juvenile delinquency is definitely a problem with which the police must be concerned. The involvement of children in crime is becoming greater each year to the extent that the commission of certain crimes is dominated by juveniles. For

---

[1] Raymond B. Fosdick, *American Police Systems* (New York: The Century Company, 1920), p. 356.

example, the 1971 Uniform Crime Reports published by the Federal Bureau of Investigation indicated that young persons under eighteen accounted for 52 percent of all arrests for burglary, 56 percent of all arrests for auto theft, and 33 percent of all arrests for robbery.[2]

Nearly every police department needs a working unit staffed with carefully selected and qualified officers who will devote nearly all of their working time to the juvenile problem. These men should have special training and education in such things as crime causation, adolescent psychology, child growth and development, human relations, and the handling of juveniles. They must also, of course, have a sincere interest in children and be dedicated to helping them. The need for such a unit will depend not so much upon the size of the department, but instead upon the number of juveniles who come to the attention of the department. Influential also is the severity and frequency of the offenses committed by them.

Juvenile problems encountered by patrol officers should be referred to the juvenile bureau for additional followup. The juvenile officer should take full charge at this point in terms of working with the juveniles, the juveniles' parents, and with the other public service agencies that may be involved. Although juvenile officers must be concerned with possible criminal charges, they should also be very actively concerned with rehabilitation. Juvenile officers are in a good position to make recommendations to juvenile courts, and it is, therefore, important that their primary concern be with reintegration.

It is very important that the juvenile bureau does not isolate itself from other public service agencies. Juvenile delinquency is a community problem, and as such community involvement can best achieve results. Juvenile officers should coordinate their work with other juvenile authorities and share with them all information that is available. Full coop-

[2] Federal Bureau of Investigation, United States Department of Justice, *Uniform Crime Reports for the United States, 1970* (Washington, D. C.: Government Printing Office), pp. 18–30.

127

eration by all will certainly strengthen the juvenile delinquency prevention effort. Working in isolation not only achieves less, but it builds animosity from other agencies, which contributes to a lack of achievement.

COMMUNITY RELATIONS

Citizen hostility toward the police is every bit as disruptive of peace and order as police indifference to or mistreatment of citizens. Citizens, particularly those of the ghetto, will not receive adequate police protection until the police accept them as true citizens and appreciate them as individuals. Conversely, the police will not be able to achieve any kind of success unless the citizens appreciate the police role, trust them, and cooperate toward the achievement of the police goal. Basically, both the citizens and the police must recognize that the police goal is really a community goal.

It is quite obvious that this cooperative atmosphere does not exist and, in fact, that a great deal of hostility and distrust between the police and ghetto residents does exist. The responsibility of improving this state of affairs must rest with the police. As public servants, it is their responsibility to do all that is possible to control crime and protect the community.

Community relations is, of course, the responsibility of every police officer. Every officer must perform his duty with the interest of every citizen in mind without showing favoritism or animosity. Every officer must be knowledgeable in human relations, respect his fellow man, and conduct himself in a manner that enhances mutual respect.

However, the police officer cannot do the job by himself. This problem is so urgent that a specialized unit, where department size allows, is a valuable asset to meeting the police responsibility. The community relations unit should be an integral part of the department and should have a voice in decisions affecting the community. The community relations unit should be a full-scale operation, and it should concern itself with long-range plans that will reduce racial tensions within their communities.

It is also very important that the community relations unit become involved with the community, gain their respect, and become a respected friend to the residents. Only total involvement by the unit with both the police agency and the community will lead to any degree of success.

COMMUNITY ORGANIZATIONS

There are many community or civil organizations whose primary interests are to improve the community within which they live. As such, their basic concerns are somewhat synonymous with the concerns of the police. It is, therefore, reasonable to expect the police to become actively involved in such organizations. This does not merely mean a response to give a speech and then fade from the scene. It means involvement in the organization to the extent of participation in its activities and perhaps the provision of leadership from time to time.

There is probably no better way for the police to relate to the community than through membership in local organizations. Whether this membership is as a citizen or as a police officer, the police organization is represented and a better understanding and appreciation of the organization will prevail.

Participation in community activities also gives the police officer an opportunity to be a citizen as well as a policeman. Too often the police isolate themselves from their citizen role and consequently fail to appreciate the concerns and beliefs of most citizens.

It is a well-known fact that police effectiveness is highly dependent upon public cooperation in reporting crimes and serving as witnesses. A better understanding between the two establishments will certainly encourage a climate of participation.

PUBLIC EDUCATION

Unfortunately, a large segment of our population is totally unaware of the police role, how it affects them, and what their responsibilities as citizens are relative to crime control. Quite definitely, if the public were knowledgeable about law enforcement, they would better appreciate the police and their problems. Better understanding should ultimately improve citizen-police relationships, and a combined effort would aid the fight against crime.

The police are responsible for the publics lack of understanding and awareness of the law enforcement role. Public education can occur through various media such as television, radio, newspapers, pamphlets, and presentations to schools, civic organizations, and professional groups. This responsibility may very well be assigned to the community relations unit, but all other units of the police department should participate as well. For example, the community relations unit should have a speakers' bureau that utilizes many officers in many divisions of the police agency. The traffic unit should develop special safety programs for school children, and the juvenile divisions should participate in recreational programs.

A good means of public education is a yearly "open house" that allows the public to tour the police facilities. Of course, the facilities should always be open to public tours, and the police should encourage groups to visit. There are many means by which the police can educate the public, and every police department should use every means that is applicable to its situation.

COORDINATION WITH OTHER PUBLIC SERVICE AGENCIES

There are many public service agencies and functions that are directly involved in crime-curbing activities. However, like the police, they resist change. These agencies do not tend to coordinate their activities. The police may look upon the parole people with distrust. The parole people accuse the police of harassment of their charges. The police charge the courts with too much leniency. Social welfare agencies are accused of coddling, etc. All of this leads to dissension, and very little is accomplished for their clientele. The police work with the same people as do parole agencies, probation agencies, and to a large degree social welfare agencies. All are after the same result: the reduction of the number of individuals involved in criminal offenses.

It would seem obvious that these agencies should work in close cooperation with each other rather than in isolation. Each must understand and appreciate the role of the other, and all must recognize the similarities of their roles. It might be wise for these agencies to form a council with representation from all to discuss how coordination and cooperation can better exist. This council could also discuss specific problems and strive toward solutions collectively.

What must be recognized is that all public service institutions to a large degree serve the same clientele with the same objective in mind: to help each citizen be a respectable member of society. Isolation of the many agencies will accomplish little, but coordination will increase the efficiency of all.

CRIMINAL INVESTIGATION

The investigation of crime becomes necessary when patrol has failed as a deterrent, or has been unable to apprehend the criminal immediately after the commission of a crime. The purpose of investigation is to identify, locate, arrest, and help prosecute offenders. Generally, the detective goes to work "after the fact" and must rely on such things as physical evidence, witnesses, and information obtained from various sources. As a general rule, the detective works in civilian

Burglary investigation in progress

Courtesy of Harrisburg Police Department
Harrisburg, Pa.

clothing so that he is inconspicuous as he moves about the community in the pursuance of his task.

Unlike patrol officers, detectives are not usually involved in crime prevention but with the repression of crime through subsequent arrest of offenders. Briefly stated, the detective becomes involved in such activities as searching crime scenes, securing physical evidence, interviewing witnesses, interrogating suspects, obtaining warrants of arrest, arresting suspects, preparing written reports for prosecution, and testifying in court.

132

THE DETECTIVE

The term *detective* is used to identify that police officer who has been assigned the specialized task of investigating crimes that have been committed. In most cities, the detective is selected from the patrol force as a reward for good service as a patrol officer. In many police departments it is considered a promotion and quite often the position of detective is a rank and may demand a higher salary. By having rank the detective achieves tenure and thereby cannot be removed except for gross misconduct. These practices are unsound for several reasons.

Success as a patrol officer does not necessarily indicate proficiencies that are necessary to be a good detective. It may very well be that the good patrol officer will not be a good detective. It is also true that a poor patrol officer may possess attributes that would make him a good detective. The police should ask themselves what it is that a man learns on patrol that would make him a good detective. There may be little relationship between the two tasks. Detective work must be analyzed, and patrol officers selected who possess the necessary attributes to be successful detectives.

To carry the point a little further, it may be that a man need not be a patrol officer first before becoming a detective. Perhaps a man right out of the academy possesses attributes that justify his immediate assignment as a detective. Traditionalism is the only real reason that patrol service is a prerequisite to becoming a detective.

By bestowing the rank of detective, the police department becomes unduly rigid. The position of detective should be considered an assignment for only an indefinite period of time. The need for detectives can vary from time to time, and this arrangement would allow needed flexibility. When the demands are great for detectives, a few could be temporarily assigned and then reassigned to patrol when the workload becomes normal again. Conversely, detectives could be temporarily assigned to patrol when that division has an unusual need.

Another justification for abolishing the rank of detective is that the consequent effect would allow for the men to rotate various functions. This keeps interest high among the personnel and also develops potential executives who have knowledge of the total police operation. Another advantage is that rotation of the detective function may possibly cut down on the corruption that plagues various police departments throughout the United States. The shorter tenure of detectives may not provide sufficient time for them to develop those contacts that may lead to corruption.

CRIMINALISTICS

Criminalistics applies science to aid criminal investigation. Criminalists take evidence, examine it by various methods, and then report relevant information to the detective.

The work of the criminalist involves fingerprinting, ballistics, questioned documents, restoring obliterated numbers, lie detection, spectraphotography, and microphotography. More specifically, he will analyze such things as blood and body fluid stains, soil, glass fractures, hairs, fibers, packaging material, paint, tool impressions, etc.

Laboratory evidence is very important to the detective because it can often place the suspect at the scene, prove he left something from his person at the scene, prove he took something from the scene, and so on. Criminalistics is a relatively new field, but the science is continually growing and will assume a much greater role in the future.

SPECIALIZED OR AUXILIARY SERVICES

Many specialized and auxiliary services must exist to assist the important line functions of a police department, only one of which is the crime laboratory or criminalist unit—existing solely to assist in criminal investigation.

134

Voiceprint identification in police crime laboratory

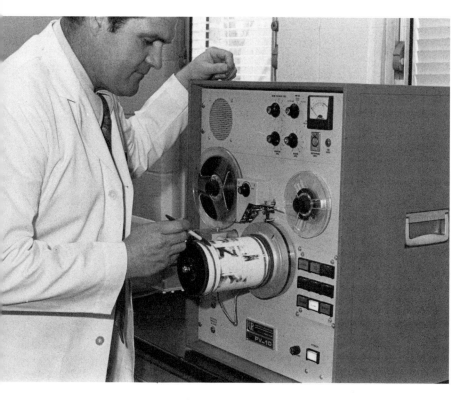

Courtesy of the Harrisburg Area Community College
Harrisburg, Pa.

The growth in complexity in police agencies has been in response to certain needs as they became obvious. When the need for follow-up investigation became apparent, the detective came into existence. When we became a nation on wheels, traffic units were established. When science became useful to police work, laboratories were established. Obviously, such development was haphazard, and the simple organizations became somewhat disorganized. The primary problem was the depletion of patrol as these specialized areas developed. This, as we know, must be guarded against. However, these are definite needs that must be met that

135

necessitate specialization or the provision of certain auxiliary services.

Necessary auxiliary services include such things as the crime laboratory, records, juvenile bureaus, jail maintenance, community relations units, communications, identification, transportation, etc. Some of these have already been discussed, while the need for others are quite obvious. Of those not previously discussed, the most important are records and communications, since the success of line functions such as patrol and investigation are completely dependent upon them.

RECORDS

Accurate, comprehensive, and detailed records are absolutely necessary for effective police administration. If a police agency expects to provide maximum police service, a records system must exist that will allow careful and detailed collection and analysis of facts and information. Such information should include such things as calls for police service, crime activity, arrests, traffic statistics, etc. In addition to the input, the information must be easily retrieved and be accessible for rapid and efficient compilation, computation, and analysis.

Centralized records not only help coordinate and direct criminal investigation but also provide information necessary for adequately determining such things as the distribution of manpower, determination of patrol areas, and determination of shift changes as they relate to called-for services. It is imperative that all incidents reported to the police be promptly and correctly recorded for current reference and review or subsequent analysis.

Records should also be kept on personnel and other administrative activities. Personnel records are of prime importance when assigning men, evaluating men for promotion, determining training needs, and improving selection procedures. Cost records are absolutely necessary in preparing future budgets. Inventory records are necessary when projecting equipment needs. Equipment performance records are helpful when determining the kind or quality of equipment to purchase.

Records systems of today have become so complex that computers and other innovative mechanisms are in broad use. In fact, records systems utilizing computers can quite accurately project future crime areas and trends which will allow better distribution of personnel. Such records can also determine within seconds if a car is stolen or if a man is wanted in conjunction with a crime.

Records are so important that the success of today's police agency is largely dependent upon their availability.

COMMUNICATIONS

Actually, there are few, if any, police activities that are not dependent upon communications of some form. For example, most citizen complaints are reported to the police by the telephone which is a basic communication medium. Patrol response to citizen complaints is a result of the receiving of such information over the two-way radio. Information from the field for specific information from records is transmitted over the radio. Communication between staff members is often via the telephone.

As can be seen, communications by mechanical means plays a very prominent role in law enforcement. In fact, a centralized radio communication system is an absolute necessity for effective patrol and coordination of effort by patrol. Quick response to crime scenes is dependent upon fast radio communication. The coordination of patrol officers engaged in a tactical approach or coverage of a crime scene is dependent upon instruction required by radio. The supervisor would find it impossible to coordinate patrol activities without the radio.

Dispatcher communicating with officers in the field

Courtesy of St. Louis Police Department
St. Louis, Mo.

Proper supervision is also dependent upon the radio, since the first line supervisor must be able to communicate with his men. Many departments have also initiated command frequencies to facilitate the supervisory function.

Like records, modern communication systems have become very complex to meet the challenging demands of modern law enforcement. Great strides are still being made in improving communications systems, and as such improvement is made the police become even more dependent upon it.

POLICE ROLE IN THE PROTECTION
OF INDIVIDUAL FREEDOM

The police, by virtue of their activity, have a very important role in the protection of individual freedom. In fact, the previously mentioned Law Enforcement Code of Ethics says specifically, "and to respect the constitutional rights of all men."

In effect, people of the community realize their civil rights through the interpretive actions of the police. In other words, police procedures and policies are in a sense telling the public what they can or cannot do. There are, of course, many controls from the federal level relative to civil rights, but implementation is the major responsibility of the local police departments, and they must be totally cognizant of the ramifications and importance of these rights.

In addition to interpretive actions defining civil rights, the police have the responsibility to instruct citizens in regard to their duties, obligations, rights, and privileges in reference to the law. They might, for example, publish pamphlets which describe the citizens' rights under the Constitution of the United States, the state, and the municipality within which they live. The police might also stress the public's responsibility in relation to those protective privileges that they have under the law.

In the past, the police preferred that the citizenry remain ignorant of certain rights since this provided great latitude for accomplishing the police task. There is no question that the police frequently denied basic rights to the accused in order to facilitate prosecution and conviction. In fact, there are those who believe such unprofessional conduct was the rule rather than the exception. Anything goes if it builds a case and convicts a violator.

As a result of such conduct, the courts—although they may have overreacted—issued decisions which placed certain legal limitations upon the police. These decisions have had an effect. They obviously limited police action, but at the same time they caused the police to take a critical look at past practices.

It is agreed that the courts have limited police operations, but *it was probably the best thing that ever happened to law enforcement*. The decisions caused the police to seek better and more efficient methods of achieving the police role, while at the same time preserving individual rights. For many years, the police had sat placidly, satisfied with age-old practices and procedures. Now to get the job done with any degree of success at all, the police had to improve themselves. The police were challenged, and it should be added that they have met this challenge and have conquered it.

The police are now concerned more than ever with individual rights, and they have accepted preservation as a primary responsibility of the police function.

Summary

Police responsibilities are more important than those assigned to any other agency within our governmental structure. The police are actually society's agents for the maintenance of harmony within the community. They are charged with the safeguarding of lives and property, the prevention of delinquency, and the protection of individual rights.

In order to meet these complex responsibilities, the role of the police has become quite broad. The most important activity is patrol, as its effectiveness will determine the success of the entire police agency. The patrol function is so basic to fulfilling the police responsibility that its goals are essentially synonymous with the total police objective .

Other important line activities of the police include crime prevention and criminal investigation. Crime prevention includes all those activities that help discourage the commission of crime. Crime prevention includes working with juveniles, special community relations programs, participation in community organizations, public education, and working with other public service agencies.

The purpose of criminal investigation is to identify, locate, arrest, and help prosecute offenders. Generally, the detective goes to work "after the fact" and must rely on such things as physical evidence, witnesses, and information obtained from various sources.

Specialized and auxiliary services must be provided by the police department to assist or support the line functions. The most important of these services are records and communications.

1. Define the police function.
2. Why is patrol considered the "backbone" of police operations?
3. What things must be considered when determining the geographical boundaries of beats?
4. What things must be considered when determining shift hours?
5. What is the relationship between patrol and crime prevention?
6. What is the role of the police in traffic regulation and control?
7. What is the relationship between patrol and the need for specialized services?
8. What is the purpose of criminal investigation, and when does it become necessary?
9. To what extent should the police be involved in the problem of juvenile delinquency?
10. What is criminalistics, and what is its role in law enforcement?

5

Dilemmas of
Law Enforcement

There are two broad, general categories of problems that relate to law enforcement agencies. First, there are the basic problems that necessitate law enforcemnt agencies: primarily the existence of crime and traffic congestion. Secondly, there are the multitude of problems that hamper the police as they attempt to resolve crime and traffic problems. These problems include such things as a fragmented police system, adverse political influence, confining legal restrictions, social disorder, and a poor police image.

In a sense, by trying to resolve the first category of problems, the police are actually striving to work themselves out of a job. Of course, such success is virtually unachievable in a society of increasing complexities and commensurate problems. *Man being what he is, there will always be a need for the police.* Even if the police were able to completely resolve existing problems, man would probably create new ones, and assign the task of solving them to the police.

Those problems that created and support the need for the police are a tribute to man's inability to handle his own affairs and to live in harmony with his neighbors. The existence of law enforcement agencies and their size are actually a measure of man's failure. In reality, Americans should feel embarrassment over the need for and reliance upon the police. The larger the police agency in relation to the size of the community, the greater the indication that man has relegated his own responsibilities and, concurrently, the greater his failure. This is true whether size is a result of the amount of crime or a result of police inefficiency in combating it, since the public must be interested in their police and must insist on efficient police service.

All this does not mean that the people should avoid having police agencies, because they are a necessary segment of our increasingly complex society. Just as the police cannot be entirely successful, it is also impossible for man to manage his affairs to the extent that enforcement agencies are not necessary. There are too many people and too many problems to permit this achievement of Utopia. It does mean, however, that man should be concerned with this yardstick of his failure and cooperate more fully with the police in keeping crime and disorder at a minimal level. The more fully the people cooperate, the more successful and less needed will be the police.

In addition to giving their cooperation, citizens must also demand efficiency of the police. Citizens should be aware of police practices, evaluate them, and offer criticism when necessary. In our dynamic society debate and controversy are indications of health, since conflicting ideas are the very essence of a free society. Of course, this is not an endorsement of illegal demonstrations, and such criticism must be of a constructive nature and voiced through the legitimate channels. Dissenters must be willing to compromise and pool their ideas through cooperative and intelligent thinking.

The police cannot completely fulfill their major function unless the people they serve act as catalysts, forcing the police to reevaluate their philosophies and formulate new viewpoints that are appropriate to the times. This citizen-police cooperative technique will help destroy outmoded customs and techniques. There must exist an ever-evolving synthesis of old and new so that harmony will exist along with progress.

Many of the problems that hamper the police in the achievement of their objectives are also a result of man's nature. Man's desire for power has often led politicians to inaugurate and perpetuate undesirable practices in the police agency. For example, to gain votes the politician may obtain help from many people and then reward them by appointments to the police force. Man's greed for money has also allowed graft and corruption to exist. And, finally, man's disinterest in basic concepts of democracy has allowed some police agencies to become lawless and careless in their activities.

THE CRIME PROBLEM

The word *crime* is somewhat of a blanket term and can be subdivided into several different parts depending upon the situation and the subject under discussion. There are basically three broad identifiable types of crime: 1) *street crime*, 2) *white collar crime*, 3) *organized crime*. Crime is also categorized into two classifications: 1) *misdemeanors* and 2) *felonies*. Street crime can again be subdivided into: 1) *crime against the person*, and 2) *crime against property*. Crime can also be broken down into specific crimes such as robbery, murder, rape, etc. The following definitions will clarify these divisions and subdivisions.

1. *Street crime* refers to those crimes that are most obvious and troublesome to the citizens of the community and, therefore, those the police most vigorously attack. Street crimes are those usually thought of when the crime problem is discussed. This category includes all crime not specified as white collar or not committed on an organized basis.

2. *White collar crimes* are crimes that are related to the occupational positions that people have. They are committed in the course of performing activities of particular occupations and exist as opportunities available only to people of those occupations. Usually white collar crime is thought of as being committed by persons of high social status as differentiated from those committed by lower social class persons.[1] Examples of white collar crime includes such things as misappropriation of funds by an executive, the use of defective materials by a contractor, and price fixing.

3. *Organized crime* bears a resemblance to the workings of a business operation. It involves a large number of criminals working in well-organized, highly structured operations engaged in activities involving the supplying of illegal goods and services to cooperative customers. Organized crime is the organizing of illegal operations involving such things as gambling, narcotics, and prostitution. Frequently, it also involves infiltration into legitimate business and labor unions.[2]

---

[1] President's Commission on Law Enforcement and Administration of Justice, *The Challenge of Crime in a Free Society* (Washington, D. C.: Government Printing Office, 1967), p. 47.

[2] President's Commission on Law Enforcement and Administration of Justice, *Task Force Report: Crime and Its Impact—An Assessment* (Washington, D. C.: Government Printing Office, 1967), p. 100.

147

4. *Felonies* are the most serious crimes and usually impose penalties of death or one or more years imprisonment in a state or federal prison. Murder, forcible rape, robbery, aggravated assault, burglary, grand larceny, and auto theft are all examples of felonies.

5. *Misdemeanors* are all offenses of a less serious nature than the felony. This classification includes such misdemeanants as petit larceny, disorderly conduct, traffic violations, etc. Punishment is usually a fine and/or confinement in a city or county jail for periods not exceeding one year.

6. *Crimes against the person* are crimes of a violent nature and impose physical harm or force upon a victim. Crimes within this category specifically include murder, negligent manslaughter, forcible rape, aggravated assault, and robbery.

7. *Crimes against property* are directed toward the illegal acquisition of property rather than the infliction of injury upon a person. Crimes against property specifically include burglary, larceny, and auto theft. Although the criminal's purpose is not to inflict injury upon a person, such potential is always imminent.

In addition to these categories or broad classifications, there are a multitude or specific offenses ranging from murder to drunkenness. In fact, there are so many offenses that the Federal Bureau of Investigation (FBI) in reporting crime on a national level has developed a measurement index that includes only seven of the most frequent and serious street crimes which are known as *Part I* offenses. These are murder, forcible rape, robbery, aggravated assault, burglary, larceny $50 and over in value (referred to as grand larceny in this book), and auto theft. The definitions of these offenses may vary from state to state, but the following definitions seem to be as nearly uniform as possible. Definitions of other offenses appear in the appendix and should be reviewed.

1. *Murder* is the unlawful and willful killing of a human being by another with malice aforethought, either expressed or implied.

2. *Forcible rape* is the unlawful carnal knowledge of a woman by a man forcibly and against her will. For report-

ing purposes, the FBI also includes assault to rape and attempted rape.

3. *Robbery* is the felonious taking of personal property in the possession of another from his person or immediate presence and against his will, accomplished by means of force or fear. Specifically, this includes strong-arm robbery, stick-ups, armed robbery, assault to rob, and attempt to rob.

4. *Aggravated assault* is assault that is more serious than common assault. Assault is defined as an intentional, unlawful offer of corporal injury to another by force or force unlawfully directed toward the person of another under such circumstances as to create well-founded fear of imminent peril coupled with apparent present ability to execute attempt if not prevented. The FBI Uniform Crime Report specifically defines aggravated assault as assault with intent to kill or for the purpose of inflicting severe bodily injury by shooting, cutting, stabbing, maiming, poisoning, scalding, or by the use of acids.

5. *Burglary* is the breaking and entering or any unlawful entry of a building or dwelling with the intent to commit a felony or theft therein.

6. *Grand larceny* is the felonious stealing of another's property when the value of such property is $50 or more. For FBI uniform crime reporting purposes, grand larceny also includes the theft of bicycles, automobile accessories, shoplifting, and pocket-picking. The Federal Bureau of Investigation includes larceny of $50 or more as a Part I offense. In differentiating between a felony and a misdemeanor, some states use the figure of $100 or more, while others use the figure of $50.

7. *Auto theft* is the stealing or driving away of an automobile belonging to another person. This usually excludes the taking for temporary use when actually returned by the taker or unauthorized use by those having lawful access to the vehicle.

STREET CRIME

Crime on this nation's streets is one of the most critical problems Americans have ever faced. Certainly, a certain amount of crime is seemingly unavoidable and has always been with us. Alarming, however, is disproportionate increase in incidents of violence and criminality. The risk of falling victim to a criminal act is greater with each passing year, and the ratio of crimes per population category has continually increased.

A quick glance at any newspaper will illustrate not only that crime is prevalent but also that citizens are justifiably concerned. Every day these papers carry a multitude of stories with headlines such as "Two Men Face Narcotics Charges," "$130 Taken in Finance Holdup," "Juvenile Arrested after High Speed Chase," "City Hit by Racial Unrest," "More Crime— Fewer Convicts," "Fifteen Indicted by Grand Jury," "Youth Sentenced for Rape," "Man Is Convicted for Murder," "Troops Patrol City," etc.

The prevention and control of crime is one of the many responsibilities assigned to the police. We might infer from this that the extent of street crime is a measure of police efficiency. If crime is rampant, then police efficiency and effectiveness must be improved. Conversely, the absence of crime or a low crime rate is an indication of police success. Of course, crime control is not only a police responsibility. It is also a function of the entire criminal justice system and of all people. However, the police are much closer to the problem since they are on the streets and will usually make the first contact with a crime or with the criminal. They play a paramount role, and to do their job adequately, they must be knowledgeable about crime, its extent, and related sociological factors.

Extent of crime. The exact extent of crime in the United States is impossible to determine. Many police departments compile crime statistics, but there are many offenses that never come to their attention. Complaints received directly by prosecutors may not become part of statistics gathered by the police. Many crimes are not reported by citizens. Available police statistics are also not always reliable since a department may adjust their figures to present a favorable picture. And, finally, not all police departments compile statistics and, therefore, an overall national picture may be impossible to obtain.

The most reliable crime statistics are those gathered by the Federal Bureau of Investigation and published in their Uniform Crime Report (UCR). The need for a nationwide view of crime was recognized many years ago and the UCR program was initiated in 1930 on the basis of uniform classification developed by the International Association of Chiefs of Police. The FBI has since served as the national clearinghouse for the program and has yearly compiled the extent and distribution of crime in the United States. The UCR statistics are, of course, dependent upon the information provided by local police agencies and reflect voluntary reports provided by them.

The UCR is incomplete also because only seven types of serious crimes are reported. As previously stated, these crimes are murder, forcible rape, robbery, aggravated assault, burglary, larceny $50.00 and over, and auto theft.

The ever-increasing occurrence of reported crime is clearly illustrated by the following table that reflects information from the 1970 UCR reports.

TABLE 1. COMPARISON OF REPORTED MAJOR CRIMES FOR THE YEARS 1965 THROUGH 1970 AND CORRESPONDING RATE PER 100,000 INHABITANTS[3]

Year	Total crimes reported	Rate per 100,000 inhabitants	Crimes against persons	Crimes against property
1965	2,930,200	1,511.9	383,100	2,547,200
1966	3,264,200	1,666.6	425,400	2,838,800
1967	3,802,300	1,921.7	494,600	3,307,700
1968	4,466,600	2,234.8	588,800	3,877,700
1969	5,001,400	2,476.9	655,100	4,346,400
1970	5,568,200	2,740.5	731,400	4,836,800

Although the information in Table 1 may not be statistically pure due to limitations in the collection of data, it is sufficiently complete to indicate the trend of increasing

[3] Federal Bureau of Investigation, *Uniform Crime Reports—1970* (Washington, D. C.: Government Printing Office, 1970), p. 65.

crime. In fact, the table illustrates that the crime rate per 100,000 inhabitants increased from 1,511.9 in 1965 to 2,740.5 in 1970.

More revealing is the relationship of crime to population which indicates that crime is increasing faster than the population. For example, from 1960 to 1970 the population of the United States increased by about 10 percent while the percentage change in crime was 176.4+. During the same period, the national crime rate, or the risk of falling victim to a crime, had a percentage change of 143.9+.[4] The greatest and most frightening concern of citizens is this probability of being personally attacked. In the United States the risk of being a victim is better than one in four hundred. The risk is much greater for people living in urban areas, as crimes per unit are highest in the larger population centers.

Unreported crime. Although available crime statistics indicate considerable crime, they do not begin to indicate the full amount. UCR totals are based on reported crimes, but there are many crimes that are not reported to the police. The extent of unreported crime is impossible to determine, but surveys conducted by President Johnson's Commission on Law Enforcement and the Administration of Justice revealed that the actual amount of crime in the United States was several times that reported in the UCR.

These surveys indicated that the amount of personal injury crime was almost twice the UCR rate and the amount of property crime more than twice as much as the UCR rate for individuals. Forcible rapes were more than three and one-half times the reported rate, burglaries three times, aggravated assaults and larcenies of $50 and over more than double, and robbery 50 percent greater than the reported rate.[5]

Even these rates probably do not illustrate the actual amount of crime. The surveys were conducted by contacting

[4] Federal Bureau of Investigation.

[5] President's Commission on Law Enforcement and Administration of Justice, *The Challenge of Crime in a Free Society*, p. 21.

a single member of households who answered for the whole family. Conceivably, unknown to the respondent, there may have been other family members victimized. It is likely that the combination of UCR and results of these surveys still underestimates the actual amount of crime.

Of interest are the reasons given for not reporting crime to the police. The most frequent explanation was that the police could not do anything anyway. This could indicate that the citizens had little faith in their police, but also it may be rationalization as well. In any event, it does indicate that the police must demonstrate an ability to handle reported offenses and must also educate the public about their availability and willingness to help. The second most frequent reason given was that it was a personal matter, or that the victim did not want to get the offender in trouble. This reason is quite understandable in those cases where the crime involved other family members or close associates of the victim.[6]

Crimes against the person. The most serious crimes and those for which we show most concern are those involving violence against the person (murder, rape, robbery, assault). These crimes involve the infliction of bodily harm or the threatened use of force with the ability to carry out the threat.

Murder is usually considered the most serious crime, and in 1970, there were an estimated 15,810 *murders* in the United States or 7.8 victims per 100,000 population. Firearms are the most predominant weapons used in murders and have been almost since their invention. Seemingly, firearms usually account for over half of all murders.[7]

Generally speaking, the police are powerless to prevent a large number of the murders, since most of them are committed by relatives or acquaintances of the victim. The police, powerless to influence family situations, are unable to

[6] President's Commission, *The Challenge of Crime.*
[7] Federal Bureau of Investigation, pp. 7–8.

153

prevent such violence. A large percentage of murders result from romantic triangles or lovers' quarrels, and such problems are usually not a police concern until the actual crime is committed.

The police are more successful in clearing or solving a higher percentage of murders than any other crime index offense. This is partially due to the high percentage of family unit murders, since the murderer is frequently readily identified. In addition, since there are so many romantic triangle murders, the police can direct their efforts toward such a possibility and frequently locate a suspect. The great success in solving murders must also be attributed to the seriousness of the offense which dictates full police action and interest. The public is much more concerned with this type offense, and, therefore, the police react by devoting considerable time and energy to such cases.

Forcible rape is the crime which is ranked second only to murder in seriousness. As with all crimes, the reported number of rapes has continually increased and in 1970, 37,720 such offenses were reported. In relation to population, a reported thirty-six out of every 100,000 women fell victim to a rapist.[8]

Aggravated assault, which includes unsuccessful murder attempts, accounts for the second largest number of offenses against the person. Most aggravated assaults also occur within the family unit or among acquaintances and are, therefore, difficult for the police to prevent. Again, a firearm is the weapon most frequently used. The use of personal weapons such as hands, fists, and feet usually account for about one-fourth of the offenses. Law enforcement agencies frequently have difficulty getting conviction for this crime because of the close family relationship between victims and assailants and, consequently, the victim's frequent unwillingness to cooperate or testify for the prosecution. In 1970, there were an estimated 329,940 aggravated assaults, a crime rate of 162 per 100,000 population.[9]

---

[8] Federal Bureau of Investigation, pp. 12–14.
[9] Federal Bureau of Investigation, p. 10.

Robbery is the most frequent of the crimes against the person, and involves the stealing or taking of anything of value from the person by use of force or threat of force. This offense usually comprises more than one-third of the crimes of violence, and robberies seem to occur most frequently during the winter months. Like other crimes of violence, robbery is primarily a big city problem, with the largest increases occurring within the urban centers. In 1970, 55 percent of the robberies were committed on the street. Bank robbery is also increasing at an alarming rate, as evidenced by a 409 percent increase since 1960. During 1969, the average bank robbery dollar loss was in excess of $4,000. Between 1960 and 1970, gas or service station holdups increased by 230 percent, and chain store robberies by 389 percent. More than half the robberies involved the use of firearms. During 1970, the average loss in all robberies was $235 for a total loss of approximately 86 million dollars. The police were successful in solving about 29 percent of all robberies committed in 1970.[10]

Crimes against property. Generally speaking, crimes against property, or theft, are crimes of opportunity and are committed when criminals think they can get away with it. The police are not as successful in clearing crimes against property as they are in clearing crimes of violence. There are several reasons for this. Probably the most influencing factor is the lack of face-to-face confrontation between the victim and criminal in property crimes. In violent crimes, the victim is usually able to provide a description of the criminal and his actions which will aid the police, while property crimes involve the "sneak" element since the perpetrator is usually not seen. A second factor is that property crimes are considered less serious by both the public and the police. The police, therefore, direct less attention to property crimes and more attention to the violent crimes. Because of these and other factors, the odds of getting away with a theft are quite good. It is for this reason that some men become professional

[10] Federal Bureau of Investigation, pp. 15–18.

155

criminals and make their living from stealing. These criminals are well aware of the odds in their favor, and become very competent in their profession.

Burglary is the most frequently committed of the three property crimes and is the one most troublesome to the police. This crime is one of stealth and opportunity, and the burglar usually directs his attention to unattended apartments, houses, and businesses. The extent of daytime burglaries is steadily increasing but over half are committed under the cover of darkness. Because of the volume of burglary and the fact that such crimes occur almost anywhere, the police experience great difficulty in its suppression and prevention. Property loss to burglary is quite high and according to the UCR amounted to over 672 million dollars in 1970—an average dollar loss of $310 per offense.[11]

Larceny over $50 is the second most frequently occurring crime of the crime index, and in 1970 the crime rate rose to 859 offenses per 100,000 population. The average value of property stolen in 1970 was $106 for a total loss of 450 million dollars.[12] As with burglary, the police experience difficulty in suppressing and preventing the offense of larceny. The crime is one of opportunity and is usually perpetrated when the chance of apprehension is low. At the same time, many people do not report the theft or do not provide "full" information because insurance usually covers the loss. In fact, it is often the case that the victim does not want the property returned but would prefer the insurance payment. They, therefore, are likely to withhold information and not assist the police.

Auto theft is the property crime against which the police enjoy the greatest recovery success. This is largely due to the temporary theft of many automobiles and the visible means of identifying motor vehicles. Many police administrators claim the increase in auto thefts is due solely to the continually growing number of vehicles. This assumption is

[11] Federal Bureau of Investigation, p. 21.
[12] Federal Bureau of Investigation, p. 22.

refuted by statistics which indicate that the percentage increase in auto theft has continually been greater than the percentage increase in automobile registrations. Like most other crimes, auto theft is also primarily a city problem since the highest rates occur in the heavily populated or urban areas of the nation. Like the other property crimes, auto theft is also a crime of opportunity, and, therefore, the police have difficulty in apprehending auto thieves or in preventing the crime. In 1970, 921,400 motor vehicles were reported stolen, for a rate of 453 victims per 100,000 inhabitants.[13]

Other offenses. In addition to crimes against persons and property, there are a myriad of other offenses that also create adverse social problems and take up considerable police time. These offenses are reflected in the literally hundreds of city ordinances and state laws. They range from special ordinances relative to excessive noise, to juvenile hangouts, curfews, malicious mischief, washing cars on public streets, parking regulations, and then to more serious offenses such as arson and vice.

The UCR identifies these other crimes as *Part II* offenses, which include:

Assaults other than aggravated
Arson
Forgery and counterfeiting
Fraud
Embezzlement
Buying, receiving, or possessing stolen property
Vandalism
Carrying or possessing weapons
Prostitution and commercialized vice
Sex offenses other than rape and prostitution
Narcotic drug laws
Gambling
Offenses against family and children
Driving under the influence
Liquor laws

[13] Federal Bureau of Investigation, p. 28.

Drunkenness
Disorderly conduct
Vagrancy
All other offenses
Suspicion
Curfew and loitering law violations
Runaways

The thousands of arrests made for public drunkenness and disorderly conduct place an extremely heavy workload on the entire criminal justice system. These offenses take up considerable police time, clog the courts, and crowd the penal institutions. The irony is that in such offenses the only victim is the offender, and there is considerable question as to whether drunkenness should be a police concern. The emerging contention is that drunkenness is a medical or psychiatric problem, and that the police are not equipped to handle it. Rather, these people should be turned over to another authority for treatment and, hopefully, cured. The same holds true for the offense of drug abuse, which is taking more and more police effort and time to control.

Crime clearance. A crime is cleared when the offender is identified, there is sufficient evidence for prosecution, and the police actually take him into custody. A crime is also considered cleared when something beyond police control prevents formal charges against the offender even though sufficient evidence is available. Such is the case when a victim refuses to prosecute or the prosecutor's office declines to charge because a man is already being charged in another jurisdiction. In discussing crime clearances it must also be kept in mind that there is not a one-to-one relationship between persons arrested and crimes cleared. The arrest of one person may clear several cases, and conversely several persons may be arrested for involvement in the same crime.

As with crime statistics, it is impossible to accurately determine crime clearance. This is because there is no reliable way of associating the number of crimes committed with the number of offenders processed at the various stages in our criminal justice system. These proportions vary considerably, and for most of the Index crimes at least, they are quite low.

Identification and apprehension by the police is not necessarily followed by prosecution. The prosecutor may be reluctant to prosecute for a variety of reasons. The case may appear weak for prosecution purposes, the offender may be under prosecution in another jurisdiction, or other extenuating circumstances may make it impractical to try a case. Frequently, also, the prosecutor will accept a plea to a lesser offense. This complicates the crime reporting procedure and breaks down the relationship between crimes committed and convictions. In these cases, which are exceptionally frequent, the crime cleared is the one the person was arrested for rather than the one for which he was convicted.

Effects of crime.   There are many varied direct and indirect effects of crime, but the primary effects include: 1) injury to the victim, 2) hardships to the victim, 3) economic cost, and 4) fear. The most serious and direct of these is the effect on the victim of a violent and injurious attack. The likelihood of becoming a victim of a criminal attack is continually increasing. Statistics on reported index-crime occurrences indicate that the probability of being victim to a criminal attack in a given year is about one in four hundred. Of course, the potential of criminal assault varies dependent upon where a person lives. Such crimes as rape, murder, and aggravated assault are more frequent in slum areas, and, therefore, the risks of personal harm are greater than for the middle-class family living in suburban areas.

Actually the total impact on these victims is impossible to determine. Factors involved are varied in both type and degree. However, all victims suffer in terms of pain, misery, financial loss related to the period of hospitalization and treatment, cost of treatment, and psychological ramifications from the crime. On top of this must also be stacked the inconvenience and hardships of trial in the event the offender is identified, arrested, and prosecuted.

Although some crimes do not necessarily inflict physical injury to a victim, serious hardships still result. A person may be deprived of his automobile through auto theft and, consequently, be without transportation to and from work. In fact, in our mobile age the automobile is so relied upon that it can be considered an actual necessity. The loss of today's automobile can be equated in seriousness to the loss of one's horse in the early years of the West. The loss of money due to robbery or burglary also can impose considerable financial hardships upon a family that may take years to overcome. Radiating from this are also the psychological effects related to financial problems within the family unit. And there is always the inconvenience of trial in the event the offender is apprehended and prosecuted.

A third major effect of crime is its economic costs. According to the 1969 UCR Report, for example, property worth more than $869 million was stolen as a result of robberies, burglaries, and larcenies.[14] Of course, cost to the victim is not the only factor involved in determining the actual cost of crime. Not only does crime impose an economic burden upon individuals, but also it places a burden upon the community as well. The economic impact of crime must also include the cost involved in operating police agencies, insurance premiums paid by individuals and business enterprises, damage to property in perpetrating the crime of burglary, etc. Also to be considered are such things as consumer fraud that runs into the millions and such offenses as employee theft, shoplifting, arson, vandalism, embezzlement, and tax evasion.

Perhaps the heaviest impact of crime is fear. Because of the extent of crime in the United States and the citizens' awareness of the risk of becoming victim to a criminal attack, literally thousands of people are living in constant fear. There are many repercussions of fear, and we find homeowners arming themselves and equipping their homes with anti-

[14] Federal Bureau of Investigation, pp. 14–22.

burglary devices. We find women and men locking themselves in at night rather than enjoying the freedom of evening walks or attendance at recreational events. The worst effect of fear is the development of mistrust and suspicion among people. An unfriendly atmosphere has developed, particularly in urban areas, and such an environment is actually conducive to criminality.

Crime trends. As indicated by the above, crime is increasing in both volume and rate, which means that the risk to any citizen of becoming involved as a victim constantly increases. Regardless of the many factors influencing the statistical data, crime is increasing and the risk of becoming involved in or in observing a crime is greater today than it was yesterday and will be greater tomorrow than it is today.

CRIME AND THE YOUNG

Perhaps the most shocking and distressing element of the crime picture is the ever-increasing involvement of this nation's youth. In 1969, for example, 32 percent of all UCR crime Index offenses solved involved juveniles (children under the age of 18). Nationally, persons under eighteen years of age made up 26 percent of the total police arrests. Of interest and concern also is the revealing fact that the arrests for female juveniles has been increasing disproportionately to that of juvenile boys. While male arrests still outnumber female arrests, the trend indicates that these two groups are drawing more closely together in their involvement in crime. This is another indication of our troubled times.[15]

It is difficult to measure accurately how much juvenile delinquency there is, and most figures must be general estimates. However, it is estimated by many that approximately one percent of the nation's children under eighteen come to

[15] Federal Bureau of Investigation, pp. 33–35.

161

the attention of the juvenile court each year. It is further estimated that 5 percent annually come to the attention of the police.[16]

Whatever the estimates, it is obvious that juveniles are far too involved in the commission of crime. Although this is a problem of several public service agencies, the police must play a paramount role. Police juvenile bureaus must be established, policewomen must be employed, and liaison must exist between all agencies concerned and involved with children. This list would be quite exhaustive, but it would include scouting groups, boys' clubs, YMCA, YWCA, YMHA, YWHA, athletic leagues, juvenile courts, schools, church groups, and the police.

Cooperation among agencies is essential, since children of concern to one agency will also be of concern to another. For example, frequently children who come to the attention of the police are the same ones that are truant from school. It is ridiculous for each of these two publicly financed agencies to work with the child in isolation from the other agency, when so much more could be accomplished by working together.

CAUSES OF CRIME

"What causes crime?" "Why does man commit murder?" "Why does a juvenile steal an automobile?" "Why does a woman become a prostitute?" "Why do several juveniles attack and rob an old man?" There are no single or correct answers to any of these questions. Crime is the result of a complex interaction between an individual and his environment. What motivates one individual to commit a specific offense—perhaps murder—may be completely different from what influences another person to commit a similar offense. Generally speaking, to determine crime causation is to determine individual human motivation.

---

[16] John P. Kenney and Dan Pursuit, *Police Work with Juveniles* (Springfield, Ill.: Charles C Thomas, Publisher, 1962), p. 10.

162

Many crimes are caused by the victim, his activities, and his availability. Often it is said that "there is a victim for every crime." A common example is the con artist's victim who thought he had the opportunity to get rich quick. There is also the woman who, by her activities, makes herself readily available for attack and rape. The assault victim is often the person who started the fight or who agitated the offender to the point of striking. Anyone who leaves keys in his automobile for the auto thief and any homeowner who leaves his house unlocked for the burglar encourages crime. All of this means that many crimes would not have been committed were it not for the existence of an available, and oftentimes willing, victim.

Social and economic conditions are responsible for some crime. The statement "remove the slums and we will eliminate crime," though not completely true, has some merit. Crime reports indicate that crime particularly flourishes in the urban areas and especially within the slums of urban areas. It is reasonable to assume that slum characteristics such as overcrowding, poverty, and racial discrimination are conducive to criminality.

The present unequal distribution of wealth in our country contributes to crime. Since social class and values are determined by the possession of material things, people strive for possession of these goods by any means at their disposal. Thus, those who are fortunate can purchase them, but the less fortunate must either go without or obtain them illegally. This problem is further aggravated by store display windows and by television. Store displays make such goods easily available to steal, and television commercials make possession of certain things even more desirable. In addition, poverty-stricken people are well aware of what other people have, and this creates some animosity that often justifies in their minds the right to steal from the more wealthy.

Mention must also be made that many crimes are committed because some law enforcement agencies do not operate effectively. As stated before, many offenses are *crimes of opportunity*. Due to lack of effective police patrol, opportu-

163

nities will be greater. In addition, many potential criminals are really gamblers. If the law enforcement agency is ineffective, they will believe the odds are in their favor relative to the police being efficient enough to prepare adequate prosecution.

As can be seen, crime causation is a complicated phenomenon, and it involves many defined and some undefined elements. Perhaps with a better understanding of crime and its causes we could better prevent, combat, and control it.

THE CRIMINAL

A criminal is a person who is responsible for having committed a crime. He cannot be identified by appearance or by any other descriptive characteristics. Criminals represent all walks of life, age groups, and social classes. They may be eighteen or fifty, men or women, wealthy or poor, black or white, ghetto or suburban residents, laborers or professional persons, etc. The only thing criminals may have in common is the fact that they have committed a crime. However, even those having committed the same crime may not be similar in any other way whatsoever. In addition, what motivates one man to commit an offense may be completely dissimilar to what motivates another man to commit the same offense.

It is likely that everyone has the capacity and perhaps from time to time the desire to commit a law violation that would place him in the criminal category. This is especially true in our present diversified society with its multitude of laws. Generally speaking, maintaining a good law-abiding reputation is largely the ability to refrain from criminal desires and tendencies. Actually, the separation between the criminal and the mass of citizens is not distinct. The criminal has been discovered; others have committed crimes without being caught; and still many others think or have had criminal thoughts but have controlled overt acts of crime.

Criminality is really measured by degrees. A person guilty of a few minor offenses should not necessarily be con-

164

sidered a criminal. If this were not the case, practically all citizens would be considered criminals. As implied previously, our thousands of laws, ordinances, and regulations make it virtually impossible for a citizen not to commit a violation during his lifetime. To define criminality otherwise would classify the violator of a minor traffic offense as a criminal. On the other hand, persons who commit more serious crimes, especially felonies, would be considered criminals. The point where criminality begins is very hazy, and the obvious determinations are only at the extreme ends of the continuum.

Actually, when a person becomes a criminal, society as a whole must take some of the blame. Certainly the individual, unless mentally incapacitated by insanity or other reasons, is responsible for his actions. At the same time, however, society certainly failed to prevent the crime and has tolerated or allowed those conditions which are conducive to criminality to exist.

Most people believe that this country's population consists of a rather large group of law-abiding citizens and a very small group of *criminals*. This assumption or belief is totally inaccurate for several reasons. If we consider index crimes alone, the fact must be accepted that there is far too much crime and far too many criminals. Although the index crimes are the only ones for which we have measurements, there are also the thousands of "other offenses" that must be considered when determining the degree of criminality in this country. There are the unreported crimes that people observe and the crimes people have committed but which have not come to the attention of legal authorities. Recent surveys have shown that most people, when they are asked, remember having committed offenses for which they might have been sentenced if they had been apprehended. A study involving almost 1,700 people revealed that 91 percent of the respondents had committed one or more offenses for which they might have received jail or prison sentences.[17]

[17] President's Commission on Law Enforcement and Administration of Justice, *The Challenge of Crime in a Free Society*, p. 43.

Although the criminal cannot be identified by individual characteristics, national arrest statistics do provide a general profile of offenders. Generally speaking, the offender is likely to be a member of the lowest social and economic classes, poorly educated, unemployed, unmarried, and from a broken home.[18] One of the most significant factors affecting crime rates is the age composition of the population. For as long as national crime statistics have been compiled, they have shown that males between the ages of fifteen and twenty-four are the most crime-prone group in our population. Of course, the age of criminals varies considerably in relation to the type of offense. For example, offenders over twenty-four make up the great majority of persons arrested for fraud, embezzlement, gambling, drunkenness, offenses against the family, and vagrancy. For many other crimes, such as burglary and auto theft, the peak age of criminality occurs below twenty-four.[19]

The race factor is quite important in a discussion of crime and the criminal. Many more whites than blacks are arrested every year, but blacks have a significantly higher rate of arrest in every offense category except certain offenses against public order and morals.[20] Many studies have been made relative to these differences in arrest rates, but it is difficult to reach any valid conclusions.

Another important factor in criminality is the comparison between the arrests of males and females. Males are arrested nearly seven times as frequently as females for index offenses plus larceny under fifty dollars. However, this difference seems to be diminishing, and since 1960 the arrest rate for females has been increasing faster than the arrest rate for males.[21] There are many reasons for this, but one of the most influential may be that the police are less controlled by the

---

[18] President's Commission, *The Challenge of Crime*, p. 44.
[19] President's Commission, *The Challenge of Crime*.
[20] President's Commission, *The Challenge of Crime*.
[21] President's Commission, *The Challenge of Crime*.

"double standard" between male and female than they once were.

As women gain equality, the police tend to treat them as equal. In other words, the police are less likely to ignore a woman's illegal acts today than they did in past years. This is not to say that females are not continually becoming more involved in crime. However, it does mean that the increase in female arrests cannot be equated with the increase in their commission of offenses.

RECIDIVISM

The single most striking fact about offenders who have been convicted for crimes against the person and property is that a large proportion of them repeat their crimes or commit other serious offenses. Arrest, court, and prison furnish insistent testimony to the fact that these repeated offenders constitute the hard core of the crime problem. A review of several recidivism studies in the federal and various state prison systems lead to the conclusion that roughly a third of the prisoners released will be reimprisoned, usually for committing new offenses, within a five-year period. Recidivism is most frequent in property crimes such as burglary, auto theft, forgery, or larceny, and least frequent with crimes of violence.[22]

According to the 1969 UCR, of the 18,567 offenders released from the federal criminal justice system in 1963, 65 percent had been rearrested by the end of the sixth calendar year after release.[23]

All of this indicates the seriousness of recidivism and its relationship to the extent of crime on our streets. Apparently, the criminal justice system has not been effective with those persons convicted of crime, and little real rehabilitation is

[22] President's Commission, *The Challenge of Crime*, pp. 45–46.
[23] Federal Bureau of Investigation, p. 38.

achieved. Not only is the system unable to prevent crime from originally occurring, but it is unable to sufficiently influence criminals to the extent that they will reform to the degree necessary.

WHITE COLLAR CRIME

Thus far we have primarily discussed those crimes that more or less directly affect the citizen as he goes about his day-to-day activities. These are the crimes easiest for citizens to commit, and, therefore, they have the greatest visibility to all people. Concurrently, they are also the most troublesome and are the crimes to which the police direct most of their efforts. Most of the cases flowing through the courts are the result of street crimes, and the perpetrators of such crimes represent the clientele for correctional agencies.

White collar crime does not directly involve or affect people of the community, but it does have a great impact on the total assessment of crime. White collar crime is associated with a person's profession and the opportunities for criminal acts that the profession presents. Generally, white collar crime designates occupational crimes committed by persons of high status or social repute during the course of their work.

The white collar criminal is the contractor who uses cheaper materials than specified by contract, the politician who purchases land because he has prior knowledge of future purchases by his administration, the legislator who sells his vote, or the business executive who collaborates with other companies to fix prices. The list of such possible activities is quite inexhaustive, and there are practically no limitations.

Available criminal statistics give little information on the extent of white collar crime, but it is believed to be enormous. Edwin H. Sutherland conducted a study involving the corporate life histories of seventy of our largest corporations in relationship to decisions of courts and regulatory commissions under the antitrust, false advertising, patent, copyright, and labor laws. He found that 980 adverse decisions had been rendered against these corporations. His study, which included a forty-five year period, indicated that the organizations had an average of fourteen adverse decisions each.[24] This is but one study of white collar crime, but this and others indicate that white collar crime is prevalent throughout the United States. The exact amount is unknown, but its cost in dollars is probably greater than all street crimes combined. Where burglaries and robberies may involve a few hundred dollars each, white collar crimes involve many thousands of dollars.

Cost in dollars is not the only cost imposed upon society by white collar crime. In addition to financial loss, there is the cost measured in physical injury or death. The use of defective materials may cause a building to collapse, thus injuring or killing several people. Food sold in violation of the Pure Food and Drug Act may result in painful illness, which may lead to permanent disabilities or death.

Another cost attributed to white collar crime is the loss of social relations among business and individuals. Those business enterprises that flout the law set an example for other businesses to follow. It is reasonable to suspect that one corporation's involvement in illegal acts may force competitors into similar practices if they are to survive. In addition, if businessmen who are leaders in the community become involved in "shady" activities, the youth of the community may begin to believe it acceptable behavior to deviate from the law. This later situation is exemplified by the common comment that a person is a "shrewd" businessman rather than a criminal.

Finally, white collar crime violates trust among individuals and between businesses and consumers. Such mistrust demoralizes the entire community and actually perpetrates community or social disorganization.

[24] Edwin H. Sutherland, *White Collar Crime* (New York: Holt, Rinehart and Winston, Inc., 1949), p. 20.

ORGANIZED CRIME

One of the greatest, if not the greatest, problems facing the United States today is the extent of organized crime and its damaging effects on our society. If organized crime continues unchecked as it has in the past, it may very well be the element that will decay and eventually destroy our democratic heritage. Organized crime is a common enemy to all citizens from all walks of life, and its immunity from detection and prosecution must cease to exist. Citizens and the police must create a united front and an all-out war on organized crime to eliminate it from the American scene.

The Mafia, La Cosa Nostra, the Syndicate, the Organization, and the Mob, are some of the names used to identify organized crime. Whatever its name, it is the most menacing purveyor of crime in the United States. According to the late J. Edgar Hoover, "Organized crime is filth with a vile stench. It is the personification of every lawless evil. It is a cancer in our society which is being allowed to grow by some people and actively nurtured by others."[25]

La Cosa Nostra, the label given the American group of the Mafia, is a national conspiracy of thousands of men engaged in varied and dangerous full-time criminal activities. This conspiracy is well-insulated, nearly invisible, and relatively unchallenged. Organized crime is dominated by a monolithic organization of national scope and feudal makeup. It is estimated that La Cosa Nostra pockets more than half the money taken in by criminal activity in the United States. In Pennsylvania, from gambling alone, organized crime grosses an estimated 2 billion dollars a year. This is as much as the entire operating budget for the State of Pennsylvania.[26]

La Cosa Nostra operates directly, or through franchises, vast and lucrative criminal enterprises in gambling, loan sharking, untaxed liquor, narcotics, prostitution, labor rack-

[25] J. Edgar Hoover, "War on Organized Crime," *DePaul Law Review*, Vol. 16, No. 2 (1964), p. 195.

[26] Pennsylvania Crime Commission, *Task Force Report: Goals of Justice* (Harrisburg: Pennsylvania Crime Commission, 1969), p. 8.

eteering and taking over legitimate businesses. The operator of a criminal enterprise that is franchised by organized crime pays a percentage of his gross *take* to the organized crime syndicate and in return he receives *protection.* He is granted a monopoly on his activity in his locality, enforced by threats, terror, and violence directed by *La Cosa Nostra* against possible competitors. If he is harassed or arrested by the police, the experience and legal talent that *La Cosa Nostra* can marshal is used on his behalf to cope with the law. He has no choice in accepting this arrangement; any attempt to operate independently results in violent retribution from the forces of organized crime.[27]

Organized crime bases its operation on corruption, force, and fear. Attempts are made to bribe public officials so that rackets, such as gambling, prostitution, and loan sharking can flourish. In 1961, for example, such a bribery attempt was successful in one eastern Pennsylvania community. In this community, one man controlled numbers, horse betting, and a crap game bankrolled at $900,000 per week. He selected the chief of police and received a substantial kickback from that official's salary.[28]

The borrower who cannot pay back the usurious loan, and the gambler in debt to the Mob, lives in fear of losing his business or even his life. Sometimes he loses both.[29] Of even greater concern, however, is the effect that organized crime has on the lives of millions of Americans. If organized criminals paid income tax on their earnings, everybody's tax bill would go down. When a burglary occurs, the perpetrator may be a narcotics addict who has been intentionally hooked by a pusher who is dominated by *La Cosa Nostra.* When the price goes up on a specific consumer item, it may result from organized crime's attempt to gain control of that particular company by pricefixing. Much of the money organized crime accumulates comes from innumerable petty transactions: 50-

[27] Pennsylvania Crime Commission, *Task Force Report,* p. 8.
[28] Pennsylvania Crime Commission, *Task Force Report.*
[29] Pennsylvania Crime Commission, *Task Force Report.*

cent bets, $3 a month private garbage collection services, quarters dropped into racketeer-owned jukeboxes, or small price rises resulting from protection rackets.[30]

The organization of organized crime in the United States consists of twenty-four groups operating as criminal cartels in large cities across the nation. The membership is always in frequent communication with each other, and their smooth functioning is assured by a national body of overseers.

These twenty-four groups work with a control over other racket groups, whose leaders are of various ethnic derivations. In addition, the thousands of employees who perform the street-level functions of organized crimes, gambling, and other illegal activities represent a cross-section of the nation's population groups. Organized crime in its totality thus consists of these twenty-four groups allied with other racket enterprises to form a loose confederation operating in large and small cities. In the core groups, because of their permanency of form, strength of organization, and ability to control other racketeer operations, resides the power that organized crime has in America today.[31]

Each of the twenty-four groups is known as a *family* with membership varying from as many as 700 men to as few as twenty. Each family is headed by one man, normally called the "boss," whose primary functions are maintaining order and maximizing profits. Subject only to the possibility of being overruled by the National Advisory Group, which will be discussed shortly, his authority in all matters relating to his family is absolute.

Subordinate to each boss is an *underboss*, the vice-president or deputy director of the family. He collects information for the boss, relays messages to him and passes his instructions down to his own subordinates.

On the same level as the underboss, but operating in a staff capacity, is the *consiglieri*, who is a counselor or advi-

[30] President's Commission on Law Enforcement and Administration of Justice, *The Challenge of Crime in a Free Society*, p. 187.

[31] President's Commission, *The Challenge of Crime*, p. 193.

sor. Often an older member of the family who has partially retired from a career in crime, he gives advice to family members, including the boss and the underboss, and thereby enjoys considerable influence and power.

Next in line of authority are the *caporegima*. These members serve as buffers between the top members of the family and the lower echelon personnel. To maintain their insulation from the police, the leaders of the hierarchy avoid direct communication with the workers. All commands, therefore, flow back and forth through the trusted go-between or caporegima. In fulfilling this buffer capacity, the caporegima does not make decisions or assume any of the authority of his boss. Other caporegima work as chiefs of operating units and the number of men supervised varies with the size and activities of the particular family. From a business standpoint, the caporegima is analogous to a plant supervisor or sales manager.

The lowest level members of the family are the *soldati*, the soldiers who report to the caporegima. A soldier may operate a particular illicit enterprise such as loan sharking, a dice game, a lottery, or a book making operation on a commission basis, or he may own the enterprise and pay a portion of his profit to the organization in return for their protection or for the right to operate.

Beneath the soldiers in the hierarchy are large numbers of employees and commissioned agents who are not members of the family. These are the people who do most of the actual work in various enterprises. They have no buffers or other insulation from law enforcement and take bets, drive trucks, answer telephones, sell narcotics, tend the stills, and work in legitimate businesses. The structure and activities of a typical family are shown in the chart on page 174.[32]

The highest ruling body of the twenty-four families is the *Commission*. This body serves as a combination legislature, supreme court, board of directors and arbitration board; its principal functions are judicial. Family members

[32] President's Commission, *The Challenge of Crime*.

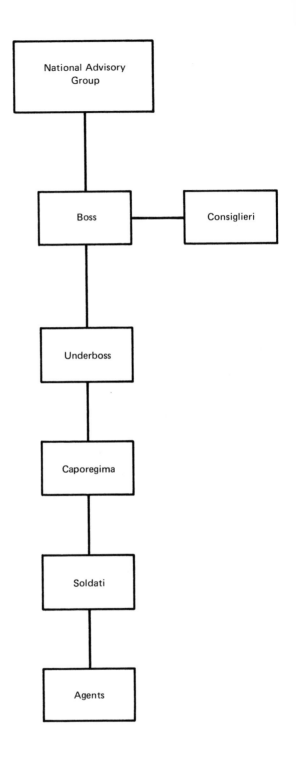

174

look to the commission as the ultimate authority on organizational and jurisdictional disputes. It is composed of the bosses of the nation's most powerful families but has authority over all twenty-four.[33]

Public agencies and governmental officials have recently become concerned about the problem of organized crime. As a result, the federal government has reinforced the organized crime unit of the United States Justice Department so that it will have a greater striking power. Many states have also initiated special law enforcement agencies to deal with organized crime. Unfortunately, the war against organized crime is in its infant stage, and it will be some time before much is realized in terms of eliminating or eradicating this problem.

THE TRAFFIC PROBLEM

The traffic problem is as old as man's first attempts to go from one place to another. Never being satisfied, man has continually searched for a faster means of reaching his destination. As he developed faster and better means of travel, he has simultaneously created problems of unparalleled magnitude. Today man has developed machines possessing power and speed beyond his needs, while he apparently does not possess the ability to adequately handle them. He has, in a sense, developed a *monster* that when improperly used leaves a trail of death, destruction, and horror.

THE TRAFFIC PICTURE

Every issue of any local newspaper will contain a multitude of stories reporting traffic accidents and the resulting deaths. Headlines read, "Playing Child Killed by Automobile," "Newsboy Struck by Auto," "Family of Six Killed in Two-Car Collision," and many similar such titles.

[33] President's Commission, *The Challenge of Crime.*

More people are killed and maimed in automobile accidents than by any other accident category. Traffic accidents alone cause more deaths and injuries than the combined totals of all other crimes. The number of men lost on the battlefields during our major wars has been minimal in comparison with the loss of lives on this nation's streets and highways. Each year there are more than 50 thousand people killed and 2 million seriously injured as a result of traffic accidents. This means that approximately one out of every 200 Americans will be killed or injured next year as a result of a traffic accident. During a person's lifetime, of course, his chances of being involved in a traffic accident become increasingly greater. In fact, one out of every two people probably can look forward to involvement in some sort of traffic accident during his or her lifetime.

It would appear that there is no letup in sight. Motor vehicle deaths and injury totals increased by more than one-fourth in the decade of the sixties as compared to the fifties. In the decade from 1950 to 1959, there were 375,000 deaths and 13,350,000 injuries, while the sixties reported 475,000 deaths and 17,200,000 injuries.[34] It is anticipated that the seventies will present an even more horrible picture in terms of traffic accident deaths and disabling injuries.

Of lesser consequence, but startling to say the least, is the economic loss due to motor vehicle accidents. At the present time this loss totals more than 12 billion dollars annually.[35] It has been estimated by some that in most communities the economic loss due to motor vehicle accidents is greater than the total police budget. More accidents and a higher cost per accident nearly doubled the economic loss from the fifties to the sixties.[36]

Most of the accidents causing death and injury result directly from violations of the rules of the road. The viola-

[34] National Safety Council, *Accident Facts: 1970* (Chicago: National Safety Council, 1971), p. 41.

[35] National Safety Council.

[36] National Safety Council.

tions most frequently causing accidents are drunk driving, speeding, failure to yield the right of way, and driving on the wrong side of the road. Of these, drunk driving and speeding contribute to the largest percentage of traffic accidents. It would seem logical for the police to particularly crack down on these two serious offenses by utilization of periodic spot checks. It certainly stands to reason the police should particularly attack those offenses which are known to be significant contributors to traffic accidents.

Every year Americans by the millions play Russian roulette on the highways, recklessly betting their lives that the spinning wheels of their automobiles won't result in death or injury. The best of automobile and highway design is of no avail if the weapon—the auto—is wielded by a reckless and careless person, and if the obvious rules of commonsense are blithely ignored by the chancetaker.

THE POLICE ROLE

As stated previously, if the police accept the responsibility of preserving lives, they must also accept the responsibility of traffic control. In fact, traffic control overshadows every other police regulatory task because it involves practically every person in the community. Automobile drivers, bicycle riders, pedestrians, the young and the old, the poor and the rich, all are affected by the diverse problems arising from the continually growing use of the automobile.

Traditionally the police have accepted a major share of this responsibility and have devoted considerable effort and time to directing traffic, enforcing traffic regulations, and investigating traffic accidents. Simply stated, the objective of the police in traffic control is *the safe and expedient movement of traffic*. This goal may sound relatively easy, but there are many ramifications that make its accomplishment quite difficult.

First, in spite of the serious consequences, people are apathetic to the traffic problem. Even though it is in their best interest to obey the rules of the road, many people dis-

177

associate themselves from becoming victim to a traffic accident. Many citizens view traffic violations as inconsequential nuisance rules that should apply only to other drivers. Such apathy certainly creates problems for the police.

The increasing number and growing use of automobiles furthers the traffic problem. Registered vehicles more than doubled over the fifties and sixties to 107 million in 1969 from about 49 million in 1950. Today motor vehicles are practically everywhere. There are few families without an automobile, and most have two or more. Americans average more than one million miles of travel over the nation's streets and highways every minute of the day.[37] The average car is driven ten thousand or more miles each year. There is every indication that automobile use will continue to grow.

During rush hours city streets are so jammed with automobiles that it is virtually impossible for the police to effectively handle them. In fact, when such congestion exists, the police must of necessity forget such things as enforcement and devote their full energies to traffic direction. Freeways and expressways are constantly being constructed, but not at a rate sufficient to keep up with the increasing number of vehicles.

As with crime, it is impossible for the police to eliminate traffic congestion and accidents. The task of the police, therefore, is to do the best they can under prevailing conditions. A conscientious effort on the part of the police does help, and it is this help that keeps the traffic picture from getting much worse. The police are not superhumans, and, therefore, can only do what is humanly possible to keep at a minimum death and destruction on our highways.

FRAGMENTED AND DUPLICATE POLICE SERVICES

According to the Federal document, *Task Force Report: The Police*, compiled by President Johnson's Commission on Law

[37] National Safety Council.

178

Enforcement and Administration of Justice, a fundamental problem confronting law enforcement today is that of fragmented crime repression efforts that result from the large

New communications center capable of securing consolidated area

Courtesy of the Baltimore Police Department
Baltimore, Md.

179

number of uncoordinated local government and law enforcement agencies. The report continues by stating that it is not uncommon to find police units working at cross purposes in trying to solve the same or similar crimes. The commission's conclusion is that formal cooperation or consolidation is an essential ingredient for improving the quality of law enforcement. A workable program of formal cooperation or consolidation for law enforcement services within a "common community of interests" is a desired goal for improving the quality of law enforcement at the local level.[38]

In metropolises the demands for police service multiply disproportionately to the actual rise in population. Such demands may exceed the capacity of the several existing police agencies. As a result, the amount of tax revenue provided for law enforcement may not be sufficient to maintain several equally proficient police agencies within the same metropolitan area.

There is little doubt that over the next few years the demands of a small-town and small-city police department will be so great that all such departments will be forced into making abrupt and drastic changes which will be both expensive and chaotic unless adequate preparation is made now to get ready for the inevitability of consolidation of formal cooperative law enforcement.

Problems experienced by several police agencies in the same metropolitan area are usually quite similar in nature and severity. Many of them are common to all American police departments, and include difficulties of recruiting and training, rising costs of operations, growing demands for additional services, dramatic increases in traffic accidents and congestion, and literally dozens of other government-orientated problems facing local police agencies. All of these common problems combined indicate a serious need to take immediate and decisive action toward consolidation or formal cooperative law enforcement.

[38] Commission on Law Enforcement and Administration of Justice, *Task Force Report: The Police* (Washington, D. C.: Government Printing Office, 1968), p. 68.

180

The duplication of law enforcement services within most metropolitan areas tends to weaken the entire law enforcement effort. Countless hours are spent by each department in the collection, preservation, and retrieval of facts and information concerning police services, whether traffic or criminal, while neighboring agencies keep and process records in much the same manner about many of the same persons and incidents. Because of manpower and equipment shortages or overages, the deployment of police personnel geographically and by time of day varies considerably from the needs experienced by the individual departments. Citizens passing through a metropolitan area frequently experience differing quantities and quality of police service as they cross political borders. Criminals understand this and are inadvertently assisted by the problem brought about by fragmented law enforcement, which perpetuates the diffuse and often confused efforts of local police agencies.

Seldom does one find an effective central clearinghouse of information regarding police activities for metropolitan areas. Departments may appear to cooperate fully; however, there is often no coordinated, single-purpose operation which provides the efficiency and effectiveness necessary for good policing. Information concerning suspects is frequently withheld from neighboring police agencies, as much accidentally as intentionally. Wanted and missing persons bulletins and similar investigative information are unavailable on many occasions because of different methods of gathering and filing information or operational procedures used in its dissemination. In the investigation of crime, which is usually of an area-wide rather than localized nature, police of a metropolitan area are greatly handicapped by such problems as differences in public policy, specific local laws and ordinances, and the size and effectiveness of their fellow police departments.

As more and more police departments become involved in solving a crime, there arises a conflict relative not only to procedures and policies, but also many times to basic philosophies. Conflicts of any nature usually are detrimental to the

181

effective provision of adequate police services, and within metropolitan areas there may be found interjurisdictional conflicts of one nature or another in all major areas of law enforcement responsibility. Areas of possible conflict in philosophy or procedures include preventative patrol and traffic enforcement, the investigation of organized crime and vice, recruiting and training police officers, the operation of detention facilities, the handling of property and evidence, the processing of records and other police related information, the handling of traffic violations, and many others. These differences may seem immaterial, or inconsequential, at first glance; however, a review of the basic responsibilities of the several law enforcement agencies may indicate that each jurisdiction may be assumed to have a common base of operations, and, generally, similar organizational goals. However, to the contrary, in many cases the methods used to achieve these goals are somewhat different. At the same time, each of the police agencies attempts in its own way to both cooperate and compete with its neighboring police departments. While not inherently bad, this frequently produces duplicated, uncoordinated, and usually inadequate efforts. The implications of the above are apparent. This situation coupled with the large number of relatively small municipalities surrounding most metropolitan areas usually contributes to higher crime rates, increased cost of police services, and disproportionate increases in traffic congestion and accidents. As these areas grow, the situation can be expected to become even more complicated and confusing, which could create additional law enforcement problems. Generally speaking, all of these problems justify the need for consolidation of police services or cooperative law enforcement.

The whole concept of consolidating police services is a new and innovative one. It is based on the premise that future demands on the police, including the development of highly sophisticated technological and professional capability, will be so exacting, so expensive, and so far-reaching that an entirely new approach to policing will be essential for the stability of the social order. Small communities will be unable to adjust for the future if their police structure remains archaic. Just as many small towns have banded together to build and administer regional high schools to provide better education for their youngsters, so too must police agencies join together to provide better, more professional, and more efficient police services for their people.

It must be recognized that before coordination and consolidation can take place, various obstacles must be overcome. One is the idea that each jurisdiction can provide at least a minimum of police service. Also legal obstacles have to be overcome. Coordination is needed and needed badly. It will lead to more effective and efficient police service; however, it must be recognized that more research must be conducted because there is not sufficient information available today to keep the public and various police units informed of the need or advantages of coordination and consolidation.

POLICE AND POLITICS

Many early police departments in the United States were characterized by corruption, incompetence, and inefficiency. Police departments became one of the favorite targets for the spoils system, and good discipline was impossible because of the political atmosphere within the ranks.

Political control of the police included such procedures as the appointment of officers for one year, the election of the chief of police, and the control of the department by local boards. Numerous attempts to remove the police from the political arena failed. One effort worthy of note was the policing of municipal agencies under state control. This occurred in New York when in 1853 a board of police commissioners was created by state law. The purpose was to eliminate the political favoritism and ward control that had dominated the department. The majority of the major cities followed suit, but this intended solution was not found to be the panacea that it was originally believed to be. Political in-

183

fluences and corruption would just move from the municipal to the state level. Today there are only a few city police departments remaining under state control.

Efforts to remove political corruption varied and none accomplished the desired goal. A landmark in the reform movement, however, was the passage of the United States Civil Service Act in 1883 which encouraged similar laws at the state and local level. Prior to civil service regulations, the employment of police personnel was by the patronage system. When a new mayor was elected, for example, he paid his political debts by appointing men to the police force. Civil service reform eliminated much of this procedure and gave impetus to the improvement of selection procedures and consequently the upgrading of police personnel.

Patronage positions are still found in state and local police agencies and it is still common practice in many cities for a new mayor to appoint his chief of police. In some cities the mayor still has the power to promote men at his will, particularly to management level positions. Such practices naturally lead to low morale among all police officers, and this adversely affects police efficiency. In addition, officers striving for advancement may rely more heavily upon political contacts and favors than upon improvement of their ability. In other words, *police involvement in politics breeds inefficiency.*

State police agencies are susceptible also to political manipulation. A common practice, for example, is for the newly elected governor to appoint his favorite as the police commissioner. Likewise, the new department head will appoint his favorites to high positions in the hierarchy even if new positions must be created. The department heads who are politically appointed may encourage additional political manipulation and favors requested by other politicians and representatives of pressure groups.

The office of sheriff is probably the most obvious example of mixing police and politics. This office was integrated into the American police system with little change from what it was in England. Today the office of sheriff is subject to popular election in almost all counties throughout the United States. Sheriff's offices have always been prone to rapid turnover of personnel, which is directly related to the election process of the sheriff and the short term of office. Again, when a new sheriff is elected he will repay political debts by appointing new deputies and promoting others already employed. A new sheriff, because of the patronage system, knows that the chief deputy under the past sheriff may not be loyal to him. Therefore, he places his own man in that position. This constant change of leadership and manipulation of the hierarchy has not been conducive to the provision of efficient police services.

The sheriff, constable, or marshall who is subject to election is definitely and necessarily involved in politics. However, appointed police chiefs, captains, and so on down the line often depend on political assistance. They may be dependent on politics to secure the position, hold security, or perhaps avoid transfer. As stated previously, this is a system built on personalities, not merit. It is unfair, breeds low morale, and fosters an inclination toward corruption.

The above discussion supports the belief that police should not be directly involved in politics. For administrative and operational effectiveness, it is necessary that the police operate without direct political interference. As a public agency, of course, police must be responsive to public needs that ideally are defined through the ballot box. It is obvious, therefore, that there must be some involvement in politics if the police department is to be adequately responsive. It is recommended, however, that this be via the ballot box with no direct association of police in politics or politics in police operations.

LEGAL RESTRICTIONS

The recognition that the police are bound by law to respect the rights of individuals has resulted from recent highly publicized Supreme Court decisions. The controversy that has arisen over these decisions has led to charges that the courts are handcuffing the police and turning offenders loose so they might strike again.

It is an established fact that criminals have been released on technicalities of the law, and this apparent injustice to society often leads the observer to overlook the possibility that justice was being served by the preservation of the individual's rights as expressed in the Constitution. Encroachment on the rights of individuals by the police and misuse of the powers vested in them is not being tolerated by the courts. For this reason, the police must be familiar with the personal liberties granted each citizen by the Constitution and must be aware of the instances where they most often need to take measures to extend these liberties to the suspect as accorded by the law. Failure to do this creates the possibility of the case being thrown out of court.

The parts of the Constitution that are most pertinent to civil liberties are the First, Fourth, Fifth, Sixth, and Fourteenth Amendments. These amendments embody the Constitution's expression of an individual's liberties and form the basis for many Supreme Court decisions.

The First Amendment is important because it allows for freedom of speech and the right of assembly. The police have to deal with the First Amendment most often in cases of public assemblies and similar situations. When the assembly or speech is unlawful the police must, of course, act to enforce the law. However, the law officer stopping a lawful assembly or speech without a good, legally substantial reason would be in violation to the provisions of this article.

The Fourth Amendment protects the citizen against unreasonable searches and seizures without probable cause. It protects individuals against unreasonable intrusions, such as might occur in wiretapping, electronic eavesdropping, and unlawful searches and misuse of search warrants. An officer searching or electronically eavesdropping without a warrant or court order is in violation of this article. He can, however, search a suspect as a protective measure, and in this respect the court has supported the "stop and frisk" laws which allow such searches. In general, the police must have a reasonable and probable cause to search a suspect or premises before any evidence found in such a search can be used in court.

The Fifth Amendment is a well-known article protecting the citizen against self-incrimination. It provides protection against the use of confessions that were obtained under coercion or duress. The well-known case of *Miranda* v. *Arizona* brought a new dimension to the subject of confessions obtained by coercion. A ruling was handed down stating that the confession of a suspect unaware of his Constitutional rights was inadmissable as evidence. The reasoning was that the uninformed suspect was subject to "psychological coercion," and that this was a violation of the Fifth Amendment. The *Miranda* decision, sensationalized by the press, has prompted almost all law enforcement agencies to inform suspects of their Constitutional rights to legal counsel and non self-incrimination as early as possible in the pursuance of an arrest or investigation.[39]

The Sixth Amendment contains two main points relative to this subject. First, the right to a "speedy trial" is guaranteed, and a delay in arraignment which allows continual interrogation may be a basis for dismissal of the case. The police should have a case prior to arrest, and they may not create a delay in arraignment to further their investigation or interrogation.[40]

The second part of the Sixth Amendment states that every defendant has a right to counsel. By recent Supreme Court decisions such as *Escobedo* v. *Illinois*, the suspect has the right to a presence of counsel when the police investigation reaches a critical stage. The reason is that a conviction may rest on the outcome of a stage of investigation, and at this critical point the suspect may require legal aid to be assured that his rights are not being abused. The Sixth Amendment, then, is important to the police because it stipu-

[39] John C. Klotter and Jacqueline R. Kanovitz, *Constitutional Law for Police, Second Edition* (Cincinnati: The W. H. Anderson Company, 1971), pp. 206–207.

[40] Klotter and Kanovitz, p. 210.

lates that the suspect must be processed through the criminal justice system with no unnecessary delays, and that he must be provided with an attorney when the law specifies that he is entitled to representation.[41]

Section I of the Fourteenth Amendment stipulates that no state may deprive any person of liberty without due process of law. This section is particularly important because it is the federal government's authority for control over local law enforcement agencies. The result of this section is that local law enforcement officials are prohibited from affecting *illegal* arrests and detentions. It also prohibits the obtaining of confessions under duress. This means that a federal court can justify enforcement of its opinion on the dissenting lower court.

These five amendments and the Supreme Court's decisions based upon them are important to the law enforcement officer because they set guidelines for his behavior in enforcing the law. Whether or not an individual agrees with the Court's Constitutional interpretation of these amendments, the most recent Supreme Court decisions have the effect of standardizing law enforcement procedures in police agencies across the nation. This standardization has a positive effect, because it promotes equal levels of enforcement, thus sustaining "the equal protection of the law" guaranteed each citizen by the Constitution.

The police officer himself must be well versed in these provisions of the Constitution. When the rights of an individual are violated, the case may be investigated, thrown out of court, and the criminal set free. The courts will not uphold a conviction based on evidence obtained through an unlawful violation of an individual's rights. Constitutional guarantees to the citizen must be upheld.

The policeman represents only the enforcement branch of the criminal justice system. He does not make the laws and is not free to interpret them. His only alternative if he is to preserve effective law enforcement is to perform his duties according to the Constitution and its interpretation, as for-

[41] Klotter and Kanovitz, pp. 282–284.

188

mulated by the Supreme Court. His position as protector of rights is deemed of paramount importance. The only legitimate police response is to enforce the law within the framework of the Constitution and the guidelines provided by the Court.

DISORDERS AND LAW ENFORCEMENT

The decade of the sixties was one of recognition for our nation; Americans were made aware that a hunger and deprivation exists in the United States. Lyndon B. Johnson stated "Until justice is blind to color, until education is unaware of race, until opportunity is unconcerned of the color of a man's skin, emancipation will be a proclamation but not a fact, to the extent that the proclamation of emancipation is not fulfilled in fact . . . we shall have fallen short of assuring the freedom to the free."[42] The decade of the sixties showed that we as a nation have fallen short.

The poverty-stricken, black ghetto resident believes that the system or establishment has failed him. In the past ten years most of our major cities with large nonwhite populations have had serious disorders, which have been termed racial. The riots, for the most part, have occurred as a direct result of some action taken by the police.

In one city, a fifteen-year-old black schoolboy was shot by an off-duty policeman as he tried to attack the officer with a knife. In another city, rumors were spread after police arrested a black man. Another city had a similar situation over the arrest of a cab driver. In city after city, some small police action became the spark that set our cities on fire. Many ghetto blacks may resent the police as the representatives of white society's authority. This may be because the police image in the black community is a bad one. The ghetto resident may believe the primary function of the police is to

[42] Lyndon B. Johnson, Address at Gettysburg, May 30, 1963.

protect property rights, and blacks have no property; thus, the police do not aid or represent the blacks but suppress them.

In speaking with civil rights leaders, it becomes apparent that the black ghetto resident is rebelling not against law enforcement officers but rather against what he sees law enforcement as representing: an inherently racist white society that attempts to maintain a position of superiority over the subservient minorities.

In the ghetto, unemployment and underemployment are common. In the schools, segregation or defacto segregation exists today—fifteen years after the *Brown* decision. Segregated schools are inherently unequal. Our welfare system is inadequate to meet the needs of the poor, and it perpetuates welfare rather than offering meaningful ways of removing people from welfare rolls to become productive members of society. Ghetto housing remains substandard and will continue to be so until a national effort is made to improve it. This continuous lack of education, meaningful employment, and adequate housing leads to family breakups, prostitution, dope addiction, and crime that leads to the jungle of insecurity and tension that the Kerner Commission talks of as being the racial ghetto.

These are the things that cause a riot, but it is the action by the police that ignites it. The police represent the ghetto's link to the establishment, and thus are seen as being repressive. The blacks believe that they have experienced police brutality and harassment, and as long as they are subject to degrading verbal abuse they will strike out at law enforcement officials.

Allegations of police brutality, accusations of differential treatment by the police of black citizens, and denunciation of police policies and practices by spokesmen for various groups have been widespread. Whether or not these charges are valid, they have been made and have influenced public opinion, creating hostility and expression of grievances. Such unrest may lead to open clashes. And that, unfortunately, is the reality with which policemen must deal.

190

There has been some indication that spokesmen for protest groups have directed deliberate harassment against police departments, police administrators, and individual officers. Usually the police have not fared well when this has occurred. The police try to combat the harassment with facts, while the public is seemingly more interested in the sensational news as presented by the protest spokesmen. In addition, objective facts usually are given in response to charges and are, therefore, too late to counteract inflammatory stories.

The vast majority of our people, whether they belong to a so-called minority group or not, have no way of assessing the accuracy of what they hear or read. Even the most objective reporting is subject to individual interpretation. It is a well-known psychological fact that people "read into" and remember those aspects of events which best fit with their attitudes and beliefs. Thus, a police action which one person may regard as brutal may to another person seem overly lenient.

The strained relations between the police and the community are evidenced by the increasing number of assaults upon officers and by the increasing tendency of bystanders to offer active resistance when officers must make arrests. In addition, there is growing reluctance to aid police by giving information about crime. Recruiting is becoming more difficult, and vacancies exist within police departments all over the country.

Compounding these difficulties is another: many officers have resigned themselves to what they believe is a hopeless situation and have taken the attitude that they will do as little as possible. Many are retiring as soon as they become eligible, and many younger men are resigning.

The role of the police is controversial with many segments of the population. In addition to the many ghetto blacks who are strongly antagonistic toward the police, there are many so-called liberals—both black and white—who feel the same. Even some ultraconservative and far-rightists are highly critical of the police, although for opposing reasons.

191

Equally discouraging and dangerous is the fact that the majority of people are more or less apathetic. The narrow views of the people at both political extremes and the apathy of the middle-of-the-roader provide a fertile field for agitators.

Within the police establishment there are two undesirable reactions to the public's hostility. First, some officers tend to meet the challenge by bending over backwards to be well liked by the community. These men, in order to avoid possible criticism, may fail to take an unpopular action that they properly should take. Secondly, other officers may react by stiffening their backs and becoming overly aggressive. Neither of these reactions coincides with the impartial and impersonal police concept of police work.

The strong possibility of further deterioration in relations between the people and their police exists. It is urgent that something be done. We do not relish the prospect of dealing at sword's point with people who should be cooperative in combating crime and delinquency. We certainly do not relish the prospect of seeing any of our community's children grow up to hate the police. The problem is ours; the need is now; and we must, therefore, take the initiative in solving it.

Citizen hostility toward the police is every bit as disruptive of peace and order as police indifference to or mistreatment of citizens. Citizens, particularly those of the ghetto, will not receive adequate police protection until the police accept them as true citizens and appreciate the police role, trust them, and cooperate toward the achievement of the police goal. Basically, both the citizens and the police must recognize that the police goal is really a community goal.

THE POLICE IMAGE

Nothing is tougher than being a police officer in our democratic society. The policeman is supposed to mediate family disputes that would tax a Supreme Court justice; maintain racial relations in a core city with little knowledge of psy-

192

chology; enforce impartially literally hundreds of laws; use great discretion such as would be expected of a clergyman; and identify the elusive criminal when little or no evidence exists. The job requires a variety of extraordinary skills that no one person could possibly possess.

In reality, the public's expectations of a policeman are far beyond anyone's capabilities. The policeman is supposed to resolve all the ill society has taken hundreds of years to develop. This impossible task is expected of the police, and when they fail in any minor way, the public is quick to condemn.

Plato praised the policeman's lofty forebearer as the *guardian of law and order* and placed him near the top of his ideal society, endowing him with special wisdom. The citizens of the United States have placed their guardians near the bottom. There is certainly a paradox; on one hand the citizens give the policeman the greatest responsibility of the society, and on the other hand place him in low esteem within the societal structure.

The police image in the United States today is a complicated subject to discuss. In order to clarify things as much as possible, a simple definition of what is meant by the term *image* is necessary. *Webster's Dictionary* defines image in several different ways. Perhaps the simplest meaning of image is stated as "visual picture that a phenomenon leaves in the mind of someone else." Using this definition, one could say the police image is a visual picture or impression that a policeman leaves in the mind of someone else.

The police in the United States do not present a favorable image today, and they never really have. It is difficult to determine exactly what their present-day image is, since perception differs according to the viewer. In other words, economic status, age group, occupational group, educational status, racial or ethnic membership, and sex all may influence a particular person's perception of the police.

Despite these differences in perception, there are a few criteria that are common to all groups. One common perception of the policeman is that of public servant. Generally, most people do not have a high regard for the public servant. They believe that public servants are less curious, less competent, less intelligent, and less industrious than those in other fields of endeavor.

Another problem related to police image is that the policeman is a faceless individual. Prior to the advent of the automobile, there was a policeman on practically every street corner. Residents saw him regularly and, therefore, could relate to him. Today the street corner policeman is almost nonexistent. The policeman today is usually seen in conjunction with his vehicle, rather than as an individual. Police uniforms also add to this faceless image: the police "all look alike."

Another image presented by the policeman is that of the "enforcer." The policeman has a difficult job because, in essence, he is the one telling people what they can and cannot do. It is very difficult to perform this function and to continue to maintain an image of respect and friendliness. People don't like to be told what they can or cannot do. People may not think much about it until a contact is made with the officer, but it is often difficult to thank a policeman when he has just cited you for going through a yellow traffic light. It is hard for the police to present a good image when so often the very nature of the job is unpleasant.

Another reason for today's tarnished police image is related to their history. Early police departments were usually corrupt and inefficient. Politics was quite often involved in the selection of officers, and this frequently continues to be true today. The history of law enforcement is marked with many ugly facades of justice. Even in this century, the police often used coercive methods to extract information from suspects. An image like this is very difficult to overcome, and older citizens especially have a tendency to remember some of these poor aspects, and some relate them to today's departments.

Some experts contend that the recent Supreme Court decisions have had an adverse affect on the police image. Take the precedent case of *Miranda* v. *Arizona* as an example. When the high court ruled that policemen must inform all suspects of their constitutional rights before questioning, many people interpreted this decision as a crackdown on unethical police methods.

The mass media is quite often responsible for today's poor police image. Television programs and motion pictures that satirize the police often are very detrimental to the police character. The news media often present a distorted picture of the police. Television coverage during civil disturbances, for example, often makes the police look more violent than the demonstrators. Magazines and newspapers often present articles that are slanted against the police.

In addition to the above list of reasons for the poor police image, there is another reason that probably contributes to this image: the conduct of the police officer in the field. He is the single most important creator of the police image. Every look, every word, every comment of the day communicates impressions to the public. The whole force is judged by what he says and how he says it.

It is important that every police officer recognize his role in developing the police image. The professional police officer must assume the task of improving the police image within his own police department. This will be accomplished if the officer is courteous, knowledgeable, compassionate, and truly interested in the welfare of others. Sincere interest will definitely communicate to those persons with whom he comes in contact. They will as a result perceive the police officer in the light that he wishes to be seen.

Summary

There are two major categories of problems related to the
police. First, there are the basic problems of crime and traffic
congestion that make the existence of law enforcement
agencies necessary. Secondly, there are the multitude of
problems that hamper the police as they attempt to solve
the problems of the first category: fragmented police services,
politics, legal restrictions, ghetto disorders, the poor police
image, and many others.

The crime problem, which includes street crime, white
collar crime, and organized crime, is probably the major
problem confronting the police, and the police devote their
greatest energies to street crime, as it is the most visible
to them and to the public. The exact extent of street crime
is not known, but the most reliable statistics are those
published by the Federal Bureau of Investigation in their
uniform crime reports (UCR). Of great concern is the fact
that the rate of crime is increasing faster than the population.
Of further significance is the revelation in recent studies that
the amount of unreported crime is about twice that reported.

There are many varied direct and indirect effects of
crime, but the primary effects include injury to the victim,
hardships to the victim, economic cost, and fear. Perhaps the
most serious is injury to the victim. The probability of
becoming victim to a criminal attack in a given year is about
one in four hundred.

The traffic problem is also devastating. In the decade
from 1950 to 1959 there were 375,000 deaths and 13,350,000
injuries, while the sixties reported 475,000 deaths and
17,200,000 injuries. The economic loss due to motor vehicle
accidents totals more than 12 billion dollars annually.

A serious problem that inhibits police efficiency is
fragmented police services. The duplication of law enforcement
services within most metropolitan areas tends to weaken the
entire law enforcement effort. The concept of consolidated

police service is based on the premise that future demands on the police will be so exacting that an entirely new approach to policing will be needed.

Involvement of police in politics or politics in police frequently breeds inefficiency. Such involvement must be kept to a minimum so that accepted administrative procedures can be utilized and professional policies established.

The police, of necessity, are restricted legally as to what they can or cannot do. These restrictions are based primarily on the First, Fourth, Fifth, Sixth, and Fourteenth Amendments to the Constitution of the United States. These amendments are important to the law enforcement officer because they set guidelines for his behavior in enforcing the law.

The police of today are faced with the problem of disorders within the cities and elsewhere. The police cannot control the things that cause a riot: poor housing, unemployment, segregation, etc., but it is often a police action that ignites the fuse.

The image of the police is not good today, and this alone creates a situation that contributes to disorder. Of course, the police image differs according to the perceiver. The poor black sees him in one light, while the wealthy white may have a completely different impression. Of importance is the fact that the police image must be improved if law enforcement is ever to enjoy a professional acceptance.

Discussion Questions

1. What are the two general categories of problems faced by law enforcement agencies? Define.
2. Discuss the scope and impact of street crime.
3. What is organized crime and what is its overall effect on society?
4. Discuss the traffic problem as it relates to police services.
5. What problems result from fragmented police services?
6. Is consolidation of police agencies feasible?
7. What is meant by police in politics and politics in police?
8. In what ways do legal restrictions benefit police efficiency?
9. How successful are the police in preventing ghetto disorders?
10. What must the police do to improve their poor image?

6

Law Enforcement
as a Career

There is probably no career with as much potential as that offered by law enforcement. The law enforcement officer serves his community, his fellow man, and gains great satisfaction from the accomplishment of his objectives: safeguarding lives and property and preservation of the public peace. Most people seek rewarding work, and there is nothing more rewarding than serving mankind. Not only does the police service offer this opportunity, but in recent years employment conditions have improved to the extent that police officers receive adequate remuneration for their efforts and dedication. In addition, each law enforcement officer has the opportunity to advance within his organization and to assume a position of leadership.

THE POLICE OFFICER

The police officer, representing the local, state, or federal government, is charged with securing compliance to the multitude of laws and regulations deemed beneficial to society. Since law is society's means of achieving conformance to desired norms, the police officer is society's agent for the maintenance of harmony within the community.

NATURE OF WORK

The hallmark of police officers is their capacity for effectively handling a large sphere of varied responsibilities.

The municipal police officer may wear a uniform and patrol a designated section of the city. On a typical day, this patrol officer may be called to a recent stabbing . . . a shooting in progress . . . a family quarrel . . . or on a complaint of a prowler. He will, of course, spend most of his time patrolling streets to insure that all laws are obeyed and to prevent crime. He will issue warnings or traffic citations to motorists who violate the law. When necessary, he will make arrests and testify in court.

The patrol officer's typical day is one of great diversity, as he never knows from one minute to the next what kind of activity or situation he may be called upon to resolve. His day is often exciting and always rewarding. Of course, there are times when the patrol officer's job is rather routine. He must perform such routines as checking buildings for burglaries, directing traffic during heavy congestion, and checking peoples' homes when they are on vacation. Important, however, is the fact that at any moment a situation may arise, without warning, where the officer must respond with immediate and positive action.

Another important duty of the patrol officer is to assist people at the scene of an accident. He must give first aid to injured persons, summon ambulances and other emergency equipment, and direct traffic to avoid additional accidents. The patrol officer conducts investigations of traffic accidents and writes reports that include such information as weather conditions and causes of the accident. He must make damage estimates and execute drawings of the accident scene. This information, of course, may be used as legal evidence if someone is prosecuted for a violation of the law.

Another important duty of the municipal patrol officer is the provision of services to motorists on the highways or city streets. For example, he may assist travelers, help change a tire, radio for road service in case of mechanical trouble, direct tourists to their destinations, and provide information about lodging, restaurants, and tourist attractions.

The patrol officer also responds to the scene of crimes committed within his beat. He is usually the first to arrive at the scene of the burglary, robbery, or even the murder. He must secure and protect the crime scene, interview witnesses, and conduct the preliminary investigation so that the detective will have necessary information upon his arrival or when he picks the investigation up following the preliminary.

202

Additional duties of the patrol officer, to mention a few, include providing traffic assistance during road repair, helping at fires and during other emergencies. He is responsible for reporting hazardous road conditions to proper authorities. Patrol officers also provide assistance during special events such as parades, celebrations, and sporting events. The police officer often checks the weights of commercial vehicles and conducts driver examinations.

The police officer may be an investigator (detective) who does not wear a uniform, since he wants to appear inconspicuous as he works throughout the community. This man investigates crimes after they have been committed. He is involved in the determination as to whether a crime has been committed, the gathering of evidence to identify the perpetrator, the identification of the perpetrator, and the long search for locating the criminal. The detective also has to prepare his cases very carefully and meticulously so that evidence presented in court will support prosecution of the offender. His is a very exacting function, as careful preparation of evidence and testimony is imperative if justice is to be served within the courts.

The police officer may ride a motorcycle as he enforces traffic rules and regulations throughout the community. He will be responsible for minimizing the number of deaths and injuries that occur on the streets of his community. He will investigate traffic accidents and prepare cases for prosecution in court. Traffic officers are experienced and specially trained so they can quickly recognize traffic problems within the community and take necessary action for resolving them.

There are also behind-the-scene police officers very seldom seen by the general public. These men generally work at headquarters keeping records or updating information that is supplied by local reports and bulletins from other cities. A behind-the-scene officer may be a photographer, an identification expert, a computer technologist working in the planning and research division of his particular department, or a criminalist working in the crime laboratory. Such specialized activities also include instruction of trainees in police schools and piloting police aircrafts.

There are also many federal agents who investigate violations of federal criminal and security statutes. For example, secret service agents within the United States Treasury Department are responsible for searching for and apprehending people responsible for counterfeiting money or federal documents. These same secret service agents may be assigned the task of protecting the President of the United States and his family. There are also federal officers with the Internal Revenue Department who are responsible for the enforcement of laws dealing with the illegal possession and distribution of narcotics. The federal officer may be an agent of the Federal Bureau of Investigation and responsible for the enforcement of many federal laws and regulations.

Regardless of his agency, the law enforcement officer has the duty of serving mankind, safeguarding lives and property, protecting the innocent against deception and the peaceful against disorder, and the general maintenance of law and order. The police are our first line of defense against subversive activities among those who wish to overthrow our government. In fact, if militant groups can abrogate the role of the police, they can make tremendous strides toward destroying our democratic way of life.

CAREER OPPORTUNITIES

A 1969 survey of 236 municipal police departments indicated a critical need for qualified law enforcement personnel in all areas of the country. It also illustrated that for qualified people who are seeking employment, the opportunities in law enforcement are almost unlimited. These 236 police agencies alone indicated that at that time they were 5,454 police officers short of what they were allowed by their municipal government. These 236 police departments indicated also that by 1975, they will need an additional 12,184 police officers.

Taking into consideration that municipal police departments are normally about 5 percent below authorized strength; that the authorized strength of police departments has increased at the rate of approximately 3 percent each year; that an average of 5.4 percent of existing personnel leave the departments each year; it is estimated that 50,000 new police officers will be needed each year in the United States. All this is to say that employment opportunities in law enforcement are excellent for qualified applicants. Of course, many applicants cannot meet the pre-entry requirements, thus the number of job applicants in many agencies exceeds the number of job openings.

Following are agencies where opportunities exist for qualified applicants. Those interested in obtaining a law enforcement position should contact that agency with which they wish to obtain employment.

Federal Agencies

      Federal Bureau of Investigation
      U.S. Immigration & Naturalization Service
      Bureau of Narcotics & Dangerous Drugs
      U.S. Bureau of Customs
      U.S. Secret Service
      Alcohol, Tobacco & Firearms Division
      U.S. Bureau of Internal Revenue
      U.S. Border Patrol
      Central Intelligence Agency
      Defense Intelligence Agency
      U.S. Army Intelligence
      Office of Naval Intelligence
      Air Force Office of Special Investigators
      Military Police Units
      U.S. Postal Inspectors
      Federal Probation & Parole

State Agencies

      State Police
      State Highway Patrols
      State Liquor Control Commissions
      State Crime Laboratories

State Probation & Parole
State Game Commission
State Inspectors

Local Agencies

Municipal Police Departments
County Sheriffs' Offices
Constables
Marshals
Municipal Crime Laboratories
Municipal Special Investigators
Business & Industry
Industrial Security
Internal Security
Insurance Claim Investigation
Private Detective Agencies

QUALIFICATIONS, TRAINING, AND ADVANCEMENT

State and local civil service regulations usually govern the appointment of police officers to the force. Therefore, candidates usually must be citizens of the United States. Other entry requirements vary from agency to agency, although frequently applicants must be twenty-one years of age. Generally speaking, the physical requirements for men entering into the police service are as follows:

1. Minimum height 5′8″ or 5′9″ to a maximum of 6′4″
2. Weight in proportion to height
3. Eyesight: 20/30 to 20/20 uncorrected
4. Age: minimum of 21, to maximum of 35

It would appear that such requirements are somewhat restrictive, but fortunately many departments are beginning to recognize the arbitrariness of these traditional standards. Many are lowering the height requirements and allowing vision as 20/20 *corrected* for each eye. There has also been a trend to lower the age requirements by employing men and women eighteen years of age as police cadets. A cadet would not normally work in a critical area and would assume tasks that present little danger to himself, tasks that can be assumed by a less experienced person.

At the present time, a high school diploma or its equivalent appears to be the standard pre-entry educational requirement of police departments throughout the United States. In a 1969 survey of 339 police agencies it was found that only twelve would hire a person with less than a high school education or its equivalent. Conversely, only ten of these 339 agencies required more than a twelfth-grade education. Seven city departments, all in western United States, required an associate degree, with one department requiring a college diploma. Although the educational entrance level is quite low, it is significant that a few police agencies are raising educational entrance requirements. Many professional police administrators believe that there is a definite trend toward upgrading the educational pre-entry level.

Many police organizations require that a prospective employee live for a certain length of time in the jurisdiction served by that organization. Again, however, there is a definite trend in many police departments throughout the United States to do away with such residence requirements. It is believed that police agencies should recruit from as large a pool as possible so they can be assured that they will obtain the best qualified people for the job. Most state police agencies, however, still require that the applicant be a resident of that particular state before he can be accepted into the police service.

Most police applicants must pass a competitive examination and meet certain physical and personal requirements. In addition, characteristics such as honesty, good judgment, and sense of responsibility are especially important in police work. Thus, most police agencies investigate an applicant's character traits and background.

In most police departments, recruits are required to complete a formal training program that may extend over a period of several weeks or months. Recruits receive classroom instruction in state laws and jurisdictions, traffic enforcement, community relations, race relations, and many other subjects. They learn to use a gun, defend themselves from attack, handle an automobile at high speeds, administer first aid, and deal with many other varied emergencies.

After gaining experience, many police officers take advanced specialized training in junior colleges and universities. More than 300 of these institutions offer programs that lead to a degree in police science, administration, law enforcement, criminology, or criminal justice. Some police agencies pay or reimburse officers' tuition costs of the courses, and many police agencies pay an additional salary to those persons obtaining a higher education.

Police officer recruits usually serve a probationary period ranging from six months to two years, and occasionally three years. After a specified period of time, police officers then become eligible for promotion. Most states have merit promotional systems that require officers to pass a competitive examination in order to qualify for the next highest rank. The typical avenue of advancement is from patrolman to sergeant, to lieutenant, to captain, to inspector, and to chief of police.

A new trend that is becoming quite common to police agencies throughout the country is establishment of a cadet program. The cadet program usually allows the employment of eighteen-year-olds in noncritical areas until they reach age twenty-one, when they become regular police officers. While cadets, they usually attend classes to learn various aspects of police work. They are also assigned clerical, communications, and other nonenforcement duties.

SELECTION PROCESS

The process for selecting police recruits varies considerably among law enforcement agencies as do the minimum prerequisites. Generally, however, the procedure is long and tedious. Depending on the agency, it may involve all or just a few of the following steps:

208

1. Application
2. Meeting prerequisite requirements
3. Fingerprinting
4. Written examination
5. Medical examination
6. Physical agility test
7. Psychiatric examination
8. Lie-detector test
9. Oral interview
10. Background investigation
11. Training
12. Probation

The order of these steps also will vary among law enforcement agencies. Generally, however, the procedures that eliminate the largest number of applicants and are the least expensive to conduct are utilized early in the process. This is quite important administratively, as larger departments must process several hundred, or even thousands, applications each year.

Police departments that recruit from throughout the United States frequently have developed a procedure for processing the applicant, with the exception of the background investigation, within one week. In this way, applicants who reside some distance from the department will not have to make several trips in order to finish the process. Usually, however, it takes much longer to complete the entire selection process.

Because of the time involved in selection, some departments allow people to file an application prior to reaching the minimum required age. For example, a nineteen-year-old may be allowed to apply even though the minimum required age for service is twenty-one. The department may actually complete the selection process and place the applicant on the eligibility list and appoint him to the department on his twenty-first birthday.

As stated previously, procedures and requirements vary considerably among law enforcement agencies. It is suggested, therefore, that police aspirants correspond directly with agencies in which they are interested.

APPLICATION

The first step to be taken by the police aspirant is the filing of an application. The application usually can be obtained by mail, although some agencies require that it be picked up in person. The requirement that it be picked up is often utilized so that the personnel office can determine the possession of prerequisite requirements before giving the application. Normally, however, information on the application is used for this determination.

There are many purposes for the application, but paramount is to obtain information that will identify qualifications for the job, information that may be used during the oral interview, and information that will assist investigators in the background investigation. The completed application also tells the reviewers something of the applicant's ability to follow instructions.

The way an application is completed may provide some insight relative to the applicant. A neat and accurate application gives the impression of a conscientious person, while a sloppy application gives the impression of a person not really interested in the job. Whether these assumptions are correct is unimportant. What is important is that conclusions are drawn from the application that make it imperative for the applicant to carefully and accurately complete the form. It is suggested that the applicant make a working copy of the application and then transfer the information to the official form.

DETERMINATION OF MINIMUM STANDARDS

The possession of these requirements can, for the most part, be determined from information on the application form. Normally, the applicant will be asked to report to the personnel office, police department, or some other designated place where he is weighed, his height is measured, and he is asked to read an eye chart. As previously stated, this also may be done when the applicant picks up the application form or turns it in.

This usually is considered a preliminary check, and the results are verified when the applicant takes the medical examination. If, however, the applicant fails to meet the minimum standards on the first check, he will be eliminated from further consideration.

FINGERPRINTING

All law enforcement agencies require that the applicant be fingerprinted so that his record can be checked. The applicant is usually fingerprinted early in the selection process, and his prints are sent to the Federal Bureau of Investigation for processing through their records. This procedure places the applicant's prints in permanent files of the FBI for future reference.

WRITTEN EXAMINATION

The written examination usually is designed to measure aptitude and general intelligence rather than prior knowledge of practices and procedures on the job. The assumption is that a person with the necessary intelligence can learn the skills, techniques, and procedures of the job. The test also is constructed on the assumption that the applicant has a minimum of a high school education and no police experience. The applicant should expect, for example, questions concerning spelling, reading, quantitative ability, word association, definitions, and general aptitude. Entrance examinations used throughout the United States are so varied that it is virtually impossible to state specific subjects that will be covered.

The written examinations of most law enforcement agencies are rather comprehensive, and the failure rate is rather high. Actually, however, any person with a sound high school education should be able to perform adequately on examinations given by most law enforcement agencies. Of

211

course, the present trend is to recruit people with college experience and, concurrent with this, the entrance examination will be constructed with such people in mind. Most federal agencies require a college degree, and their examinations reflect this requirement. Most departments also allow applicants who fail the examination the privilege of taking it over after the lapse of a specified amount of time.

MEDICAL EXAMINATION

It is obvious, due to the nature of police work, that applicants must be in good health. A law enforcement officer who is not medically fit may lose his own life or be responsible for the death of someone else.

Good health usually is verified by an examination by a physician. Some departments specify the examining doctor while others will accept a medical report from the applicant's family physician. The medical examination usually is quite comprehensive, and it is suggested that a person with a disabling medical deficiency not seek employment as a law enforcement officer. The work is physically demanding, and only the medically fit can withstand the demands of the job.

PHYSICAL AGILITY

Many tasks and activities of the law enforcement job depend on the officer's physical strength, coordination, agility, and endurance. These qualities cannot be measured in the written examination and, therefore, a physical agility test is imperative. Unfortunately, many departments do not require this particular test.

This test is designed to measure coordination, agility, and endurance rather than just brute strength. Typical components of the test are pull-ups, hurdles, sit-ups, standing broad jump, and running. As with all selection tests, the components and minimum standards of the physical agility test vary considerably among law enforcement agencies.

212

PSYCHIATRIC EXAMINATION

A recent trend in the selection process is the psychiatric examination. This examination is used to identify those applicants who are psychologically unsuited for the role of a law enforcement officer. The psychiatrist is looking for such things as emotional immaturity, sexual abnormalities, and deviate behavior patterns.

This examination is a very important part of the selection process, as it helps eliminate from the police service misfits, whose employment often creates very serious consequences. The examination also is beneficial to applicants deemed unsuitable for law enforcement work: they can direct their efforts toward other professions without wasting time on a job at which they can't be successful.

LIE DETECTOR TEST

Like the psychiatric, physical agility, and medical examinations, the lie detector test results are not given weight in determining the applicant's final overall score. Rather, the test is another qualifying element of the selection process. This test either eliminates the candidate or permits him to finish the selection process.

Many states prohibit the use of the lie detector as part of the selection process. In those states where it is not prohibited, only a few departments use it, which is probably due primarily to the cost and time involved.

The lie detector normally is used to determine the validity of facts recorded on the application and as an aid in the background investigation. Frequently, it is found that the candidate has concealed information that would have eliminated him from further consideration.

ORAL INTERVIEW

If properly administered, the oral interview can be one of the most effective means of determining a candidate's suitability

213

for law enforcement work. The oral interview is designed to evaluate the applicant's work experience, attitudes, career aspirations, personal appearance, ability to express himself, and other personal traits.

The composition of the interview board differs, but usually consists of from three to five people. Many departments include a patrolman on the board along with higher ranking police officers. It also is quite common for the board to include a person unconnected with the police service. This person might be the personnel director of a local company or someone representing a citizen's group.

The oral interview results in a score that influences the candidate's overall rating. The influence of this score on the total evaluation does differ among law enforcement agencies. Some agencies give it heavy emphasis, while others make it a small portion of the overall score.

BACKGROUND INVESTIGATION

The background investigation is another indispensable part of the selection process. There may be undesirable personal characteristics possessed by the candidate that will not be revealed by testing, but will be discovered during the background investigation. This part of the selection process is so important that many law enforcement agencies have a special unit devoting full time to this function.

The background investigation usually includes a check of the applicant's military records, high school records, references, past and present employee records, and police records from his home city. The investigators will also interview the candidate's friends, neighbors, employers, colleagues with whom he worked, distant acquaintances, teachers, relatives, and landlords. Many law enforcement agencies also have the investigator interview the candidate's spouse. It is recognized that a police officer's home situation will either adversely or favorably affect his work. A wife or husband opposed to her or his spouse going into police work would certainly place the candidate's likelihood of employment in serious doubt.

214

TRAINING

Training is usually considered part of the selection process, as officer trainees may not become sworn officers until they have graduated. Training is highly disciplined, and the academic and physical requirements are set quite high. It is reasonable to expect some police trainees to either drop out during training or fail to meet minimum physical or academic standards. Some also are not able to "stand up" under the strict discipline and stress of the training program. In reality, however, if the selection process is effective, few people will fail the training.

The extent and type of training varies considerably among law enforcement agencies. The length of such a training program, for example, will vary from one or two weeks to as long as six months. Regardless of the length, however, the purpose of training is to provide the trainee with the knowledge and skills necessary to perform the police function. The curriculum will include such subjects as firearms, criminal code, traffic code, laws of arrest, search and seizure, public relations, defensive tactics, patrol techniques, interpersonal relations, departmental rules and regulations, etc.

PROBATION

Most law enforcement agencies employ a probationary period for their new officers that generally runs from three months to one year. Basically, this means that an officer's first few months of employment are still part of the selection process. If, during this time, the "rookie" fails to meet minimum standards, he is released from the service.

This provides the department an opportunity to observe the new officer as he functions under actual working conditions. It may very well be that the officer cannot apply what he has learned in the classroom and, in spite of the previous selection steps, he is not suitable for the job. The rookie's relations with colleagues, his ability to follow instruction, his

215

rapport with citizens, and his reaction under stress all can be observed.

During the probation period the new officer is periodically evaluated by his supervisors. Evaluations are discussed with the new officer, and then placed in his personal file. At the termination of the probation period, all evaluations are reviewed, and the man either becomes a tenured officer or is released from the service. Of course, the recruit may be released also at any time during the probationary period.

Completion of probation is the last phase of the selection process which may have begun a couple years earlier. Selection is a long process, but if properly constituted it does result in better police officers and better police service.

EARNINGS AND WORKING CONDITIONS

In recent years there has been a significant increase in the remuneration received by police officers throughout the United States. Salaries are increasing to the point that many law enforcement agencies now offer a salary that is quite competitive with other employers demanding similar qualifications. In addition, police officers usually receive a regular salary increase based on experience and performance, until a specified maximum is reached. Their earnings may also increase above these levels as they are promoted to a higher rank, such as sergeant or lieutenant.

Many police agencies provide officers with uniforms, firearms, and other necessary equipment, or furnish special allowances for their purchase.

In almost all police agencies, the scheduled work week is forty hours. Police protection must be provided around the clock and, therefore, some officers are on duty over the weekends, on holidays, and at night. Of course, police officers are subject to emergency calls at any time.

Most police officers are covered by rather liberal pension plans and are able to retire at a relatively young age.

216

Paid vacations; sick leave; and medical, surgical, and life insurance plans are frequently provided.

The work of police officers is sometimes hazardous. There is always the risk of an automobile accident during pursuit of a speeding motorist or a fleeing criminal. When controlling riots and apprehending criminals, a police officer faces the risk of bodily harm. However, the risks involved in police work are not as great as most people think. For one thing, police officers are highly trained so they are capable of handling emergency and hazardous situations. For example, the risk of a traffic accident in a high speed chase is drastically minimized because police officers have been well trained to cope with such situations. In a gun battle, the police officer is usually the better shot. Police officers are also trained in protecting themselves so that the risk of bodily harm in forceable arrest is also minimized. In fact, it is suggested that the accident rate among police officers is less than that of many other occupations.

POLICE WOMEN

Today's police administrators have availed themselves and their departments of many of the advantages that have automatically come with advancement toward professional status: improved salary plans, reduced work weeks, educational and training programs, and modern equipment. However, many police officials have failed to recognize the tremendous advantages of employing policewomen.

Whether this failure is due to stratified thinking, lack of knowledge, or the determination to jealously guard the field of law enforcement from encroachment by females is relatively unimportant. What is important is that whatever the reason, as long as members of the police service fail to acknowledge the urgent need for policewomen in their individual departments, the effectiveness and efficiency of their operations will be hampered.

217

To those who continue to resist the idea of women in police work, it should be pointed out that as early as 1888 New York City appointed its first full-time police matron.

Endorsements and statistics would reveal the worldwide success of the utilization of policewomen. However, there are police officials, especially at the municipal level, who are reluctant to consider its merits, claiming that funds are meager, the department is extremely small, introduction of new programs of this kind would become the concern of the entire community. While these administrators have used these as excuses, the fact is that these should be some of the very reasons for instituting such a program.[1]

Generally speaking, women in police work are required to have a greater amount of education than their male counterparts. Other than this, however, requirements are very similar in that the woman applicant must be in excellent physical condition, have a high moral character, and meet specified weight, height, and eyesight requirements. In addition, the female applicant, like the male, must undergo a thorough background investigation.

The work of a policewoman can be quite varied and very challenging. Typically, the woman is assigned to the criminal investigation bureau where she works with juvenile offenders. Her particular interest will be directed toward the girl juveniles who have been involved in a crime. Therefore, the policewoman will investigate crimes ranging from homicide to petty larceny. The policewoman may also be called upon to conduct undercover investigations, as there are certain situations where only she can fit. For example, women often are used as decoys in apprehending purse snatchers and sex violators. Other assignments might include accompanying a male officer on stakeouts, participating in raids so that she can handle female prisoners, and certain kinds of public relations work. It must be remembered that policewomen are not equated to the role of metermaids. The po-

---

[1] Felicia Shpritzer, "A Case for the Promotion of Police Women in the City of New York." *Police*, July–August, 1961, p. 57.

licewoman is a professional police officer and normally has the same pay and fringe benefits as male counterparts. The professional policewoman also has opportunities for promotion from the rank of patrolman to lieutenant, captain, or even chief of police.

There also are many opportunities for qualified women in Federal law enforcement. All Federal investigative organizations are recruiting women. The work of women in these agencies is quite diversified and dependent upon each agency's philosophy.

In today's complex world, it is imperative that more police departments seek and employ women police officers. It is a fact that certain tasks can be better performed by women, and that certain circumstances justify the presence of a woman.

Summary

Police officers must have the unusual capacity to effectively handle a large sphere of varied activities. In any one day, a police officer may be called upon to save a child from drowning, investigate a serious traffic accident, give directions to a tourist, respond to an armed robbery, or even to inform a woman of her husband's death. Today's police officer must be carefully selected and highly trained in order to fulfill his many and awesome responsibilities.

A police officer may be assigned to patrol, serve as a detective, ride a motorcycle, or operate as a radio dispatcher. He may also be assigned to a specialized activity such as criminal identification, communications, planning and research, or working in the crime laboratory.

The need for qualified law enforcement personnel is critical. A survey of 236 police departments indicated that by 1975, they will need an additional 12,184 police officers. This clearly illustrates that employment opportunities in law enforcement are excellent for qualified applicants. These opportunities exist at all levels of government as well as with private industry and organizations.

Qualifications for police service vary from agency to agency, but generally, the requirements are a high school diploma and the meeting of certain physical requirements. Federal agencies usually require a college degree, and a few municipal agencies are raising their educational requirements beyond that of high school.

Working conditions have improved considerably over the last few years to the extent that officers now enjoy competitive salaries and fringe benefits. The trend is for the continued increase of salaries.

Opportunities for women in police work are increasing, as departments across the country are becoming cognizant of their value. Generally, women are required to have a greater amount of education than their male counterparts.

Other than this, however, requirements are similar in that women must be in excellent physical condition, have a high moral character, and meet specified weight, height, and eyesight requirements. The policewoman usually enjoys the same salary and fringe benefits as the policeman.

Discussion Questions

1. What is a policeman?
2. Describe the nature of the police officer's work.
3. How does the work of a municipal officer differ from that of a federal officer?
4. Discuss eyesight requirements for a police applicant and the trend relative to this.
5. Discuss career opportunities in law enforcement.
6. What are the general qualifications for a police applicant? Support the need for such requirements.
7. What is the fallacy of the residence requirement for a police applicant?
8. What is the purpose of the probationary period?
9. Discuss the specialized services that a police officer may perform.
10. Discuss the role of women in law enforcement.

7

Administration of Justice

The process of criminal justice involves a large number of separate and sequential steps. It involves the many activities of the police, judicial proceedings, and correctional agencies. The process begins with the commission of a crime and ends, hopefully, with rehabilitation of the offender and his return to a normal and productive life. This is, of course, an over-simplification of the process, as several activities occur sub-sequent to the commission of an offense and before the reha-bilitation of the offender. In addition, outcomes of various steps determine what will or will not follow.

For clarification and ease of understanding, the steps in the administration of justice are grouped into: 1) police proc-ess, 2) pre-trial judicial process, 3) the trial, and 4) correc-tional process.

THE POLICE PROCESS

Within the scope of the administration of justice, the police process involves the: 1) determination that a crime has been committed, 2) crime scene investigation, 3) identification of the offender, 4) arrest of the offender, 5) booking of the offender, and 6) investigation and case preparation. With the possible exception of an on-sight arrest, this represents the normal sequence of events. In an on-sight arrest, the crime scene investigation may follow the arrest, and the identifica-tion of the offender will occur simultaneously with the deter-mination that a crime actually has been committed. There may be other exceptions to this, but the above listed se-quence usually holds true.

DETERMINING THAT A CRIME HAS BEEN COMMITTED

One of the first responsibilities of the police upon arrival at the scene of a reported crime is to determine whether a crime has in fact been committed. Frequently, people call the police on the premise that "There ought to be a law." This is especially true in the case of civil disputes over which the police have no authority. Good examples are the person who calls the police because his neighbor has planted a hedge over the property line or the woman who complains about her husband's late hours.

Concurrent with determining that a crime has been committed is the decision as to what the crime is. Both determinations must be based on law. This clearly illustrates why it is imperative that police officers be knowledgeable in criminal law and know the elements of a crime.

In burglary, for example, the essential elements necessary to constitute the offense may be the *breaking* and *entering* the house of another, with *intent* to *commit* a *felony* therein. (Definition of burglary will vary among states.) All of these elements must exist before the police officer can conclude that a crime has been committed and that the crime is burglary.

This determination may not be as simple as it sounds, as there are other considerations. The officer must know the legal definitions of *breaking, entering*, and *intent*. Is it considered breaking if there is no forcible entry? Does the perpetrator have to enter with his whole person or does reaching into the premises to obtain an object constitute entering? Is intent implied if a theft has occurred? Is asportation necessary for a theft to occur? All of these questions and more must be answered before the final determination can be made.

As can be seen, the determination that a crime has been committed involves some investigatory work. In the case of burglary this would involve, among other things, discovering the means of entry and whether or not something was stolen. A good example of how the investigation determines the crime is the question of murder or suicide. Does the evidence support a suicide or does it indicate murder?

CRIME SCENE INVESTIGATION

The crime scene investigation has three general objectives: 1) to assist in determining that a crime has been committed and the identification of what the specific crime is, 2) to secure evidence that provides proof relative to the perpetration of the crime and the identity of the offender, and 3) to identify the criminal. In the case of an on-sight arrest of a criminal during the commission of a crime, these objectives are quickly and easily achieved. In other instances, however, the investigation can be quite involved and an arrest may occur weeks, months, or even years after the commission of the crime.

One crime scene investigation may involve the patrol officer who is the first to arrive, detectives who may be summoned by the patrol officer, crime-scene evidence technicians, and crime laboratory specialists. All have very important roles, and the success of the investigation is dependent upon the ability of each in the performance of his tasks. Their efforts must also be well coordinated.

In most situations, the patrol officer is the first to arrive at the crime scene, but his responsibility will vary from department to department. In some departments, he will merely protect the scene and summon detectives. In other departments, the patrol officer will conduct the entire preliminary investigation unless it is a serious crime. In a few departments, he will conduct the investigation to its conclusion. This third alternative is, however, rather rare.

It is common for the beat officer to assume major responsibility for the preliminary investigation. The preliminary investigation consists of: 1) protecting the crime scene, 2) preserving the crime scene, 3) searching the scene for evidence, 4) packaging evidence and transporting it to the crime laboratory, 5) interviewing witnesses, and 6) preparing a detailed investigation report that will be forwarded to the detective division for necessary follow-up investigation.

It should be understood that whether detectives or beat officers are responsible for the preliminary investigation they will usually utilize the service of specialists such as a police photographer and fingerprint expert. In larger departments, evidence technicians will search the scene, serve and package evidence, and transport it to the laboratory.

IDENTIFYING THE OFFENDER

As stated previously, one of the primary objectives of the investigation is the identification of the offender. In many cases, the victim can name the person responsible. This is frequently true in the case of an assault, as most assaults are committed by a person known by the victim. In other situations, however, the identification is not so easily accomplished.

Identification of the offender is usually accomplished by information given by the victim and witnesses. Frequently, the police have just descriptions to go on, but this is often sufficient. The police may be able to develop a composite from the description, or someone may be able to identify the suspect from pictures in the police file.

The offender may also be identified by physical evidence, such as fingerprints, that may be found at the scene. Admittedly, however, this means of identification is not as common as many people believe. If the offender is identified, the next step in the administration of justice is finding the responsible person and effecting the arrest.

THE ARREST

Arrest is defined as "taking, under real or assumed authority, custody of another for the purpose of holding or detaining him to answer a criminal charge or civil demand."[1] In many instances, the actual arrest is made on the scene subsequent to the commission of the crime. Frequently, however, the arrest will not be made until a thorough investigation has been made and a legal warrant issued for the arrest of the perpetrator.

There are two types of arrests: 1) with a warrant, and 2) without a warrant. A police officer can legally make an arrest without a warrant when he observes the commission of a misdemeanor or when a felony is committed and he has reasonable grounds to believe that a certain person has com-

---

[1] Henry Campbell Black, *Black's Law Dictionary* (St. Paul, Minnesota: West Publishing Company, 1951), p. 140.

mitted that felony. Police officers must know the legal status of arrest without a warrant within their particular jurisdiction, as it may vary slightly from state to state.

A warrant of arrest is defined as "a written order issued and signed by a magistrate, directed to a peace officer or some other person specially named, and commanding him to arrest the body of a person named in it, who is accused of an offense."[2] Generally, it is best if the police department can obtain a warrant of arrest prior to making an arrest, as this provides a legal document supporting that arrest. Generally, criminal investigations will end with the obtaining of a warrant that is served by a police officer.

The manner in which an arrest is accomplished will depend upon the situation. In some cases, the officer can control the conditions, but in other cases the officer must use force; in such cases the force used should be only the amount necessary to overcome the resistance of the offender.

BOOKING

Following the arrest, the suspect is taken to the jail where he is "booked." Booking refers to making positive identification of the suspect before he is actually placed in detention. This procedure consists of fingerprinting the suspect, photographing him, and verifying his name.

The booking procedure also develops additional records that show the time of arrest, the person arrested, the charge against the suspect, the name of the officer making the arrest, and additional information. These records often are of great importance during the trial of the suspect, and it is imperative that they be accurate.

INVESTIGATION AND CASE PREPARATION

The final role of the police is the continuation of the criminal investigation to ascertain all facts relative to the case for presentation in court. The final report on the case must be as complete as possible if the process of justice is to work effectively.

[2] *Ibid,* p. 141.

This phase of the process entails a close working relationship between the police and the prosecutor's office. In fact, many police departments assign one or more detectives to the prosecutor's office for the phase of the investigation. Many prosecutors also have their own investigators who work very closely with the police.

The prosecutor frequently indicates what additional information he needs and, to a degree, helps direct this phase of the investigation. The objective, obviously, is to gather information that will assist in the prosecution of the case.

This should not imply that the police concern themselves with gathering only those facts that will help convict the person charged with a crime. *The police role is to gather all facts that will assist the court in rendering a just verdict.* It may very well be that some information will actually help the defense if they are able to obtain it through cross examination. This is acceptable and good.

Police officers involved in the investigation usually will appear in court as witnesses for the prosecution. Their responsibility is to answer the prosecutor's questions as accurately as possible. All information must, of course, be based on facts that are known by the police officer. Appearing as a witness for the prosecution should not imply, however, a lack of cooperation with the defense attorney. The police have fulfilled their responsibility in the process, and it is now the court's responsibility to arrive at a just verdict. Testifying police officers must answer all questions impartially and cooperate fully with the defense attorneys if the process of justice is to work effectively.

PRE-TRIAL JUDICIAL PROCESS

DECISION TO PROSECUTE

The normal procedure is for the county or city prosecutor to receive a copy of the booking slip and subsequent field investigation report. The prosecutor has the responsibility of determining if there is sufficient evidence to bring charges against the suspect. The prosecutor, if he decides to prosecute, will prepare the complaint which contains the name of the person and the offense that the person has committed and is charged with. The complaint is usually signed by the arresting officer or complaining witness as well as by the prosecutor.

THE PRESENTMENT

The second step in the pre-trial judicial process is taking the offender before a magistrate without unnecessary delay. The magistrate then informs the suspect of the charge against him as well as his constitutional rights relative to that charge and the criminal justice procedure. He is also informed of his right for preliminary examination as well as his right to legal counsel. If the suspect is indigent, the magistrate or court may appoint counsel for him. The magistrate may also set bail at this initial appearance of the suspect.

PRELIMINARY HEARING

The preliminary hearing is not a trial for determining the guilt or innocence of the suspect, but an open hearing to determine if there is sufficient evidence to hold the accused for trial. If, in the opinion of the judge, the evidence is sufficient, the accused will be bound over for trial by a court that possesses general jurisdiction. Many people accused of a felony waive the right to a preliminary hearing, and their case automatically advances to the trial.

GRAND JURY INDICTMENT

A grand jury is a large group of jurers, usually twelve to twenty-three members, which examines accusations of criminal charges as a preliminary to the trial. The grand jury is a county institution, and hears the evidence presented by the state. Their duty is to receive complaints and accusations in criminal cases, hear the evidence presented by the state, and file bills of indictment when they are satisfied that a trial should be held.

An indictment is defined as "an accusation in writing found and presented by a grand jury, legally sworn, to the court in which it is impanelled, charging that a person therein named has done some act, or been guilty of some omission, which by law is a public offense, punishable on indictment."[3]

The use of grand juries varies considerably from state to state. It is suggested, therefore, that the reader consult his own state judicial processes to determine the activities, responsibilities, and use of the grand jury. Some states have abolished the grand jury or limited its activities.

ARRAIGNMENT

In the arraignment, the accused or defendant appears before the trial court, is informed of the crime he is charged with, and is asked to enter his plea. He may plead guilty, not guilty, or nolo contendere. Nolo contendere means that the person will not contest the charge. This is the name of a plea in a criminal action, having the same legal effect as the plea of guilty, with regard to all proceedings on the indictment, and on which the defendant may be sentenced. This plea admits, for the purposes of the case, all the facts which are well pleaded, but is not to be used as an admission elsewhere.[4]

THE TRIAL PROCESS

All people have the right to a speedy trial as guaranteed by the Sixth Amendment and the right to a trial by jury as guaranteed by the Seventh Amendment of the Constitution

[3] *Ibid*, p. 912.
[4] *Ibid*, p. 1198.

of the United States. The accused may, however, waive his right to a trial by jury and be tried by the judge. In this instance, the judge hears the evidence and decides by himself whether the accused is guilty or not guilty. Generally, the accused will receive a trial by jury and the following processes will be in effect.

JURY SELECTION

The first order of business is the selection of the jury. Both the defense attorney and the prosecutor have a specified number of "peremptory challenges," which means each can refuse prospective jurors for any reason. After twelve jurors and from one to four alternates are selected, the judge outlines their responsibilities, and the trial is ready to begin.

OPENING STATEMENTS

The purpose of the opening statements is to advise the jury of facts of the case and the issues involved. This provides the jury with a general picture of the total situation so they will better understand the evidence to be presented.

The prosecutor usually opens the case by explaining how he is going to present the case for the prosecution. He may outline the evidence to be presented that will prove the guilt of the accused. The defense attorney then gives his statements which will explain his method of action. He usually will explain how he will show the defendent innocent of the crime charged.

THE PROSECUTOR'S CASE

The prosecutor begins his case by presenting his witnesses. Witnesses for the prosecution present testimony that will support a verdict of guilty. The prosecutor begins with direct examination of his witnesses with questions that will bring out the facts in chronological order. After he has brought out all necessary information, the prosecutor rests. The defense counsel then cross-examines the prosecution's witnesses. His purpose is to challenge the witness relative to his testimony and, if possible, show where inconsistencies in testimony exist. He then rests. If the prosecutor believes it necessary, he may engage in redirect examination of the witness for material that may have been overlooked or that is new. Following the redirect, the defense can also ask additional questions.

THE DEFENSE CASE

Following the presentation of all prosecution witnesses, the defense calls its witnesses. The same procedure is used in this process, with the exception that the defense counsel asks for testimony and the witnesses are cross-examined by the prosecution. The purpose of the defense is, of course, to prove that the defendent is innocent of the charges lodged against him.

PROSECUTOR'S REBUTTAL

The prosecutor then engages in the rebuttal and may call previous or additional witnesses in order to strengthen any part of his case that may have been weakened by the defense counsel. The same order of testimony and cross-examination follows during this rebuttal.

DEFENSE SURREBUTTAL

The defense then engages in a surrebuttal and brings forth previous and additional experts and witnesses to strengthen his case. The same procedure as in the prosecutor's rebuttal is followed.

SUMMATIONS BY DEFENSE AND PROSECUTOR

The defense counsel and the prosecutor then are allowed to give their closing arguments or summations. Each reviews

234

the laws and the facts involved for the jury and summarizes the important facts of his case. Of course, each attempts to discuss the facts as they support their own interests.

INSTRUCTION TO JURY

The judge reads to the jury certain written instructions relative to the legal principles involved in the case. The judge also will explain to the jury their responsibility relative to arriving at a "true and just verdict."

DELIBERATION AND VERDICT

The jury then adjourns to a private chamber where it deliberates the facts and issues of the case. The jury elects a foreman who acts as chairman of the whole group. The jury will remain in deliberation as long as it takes to reach a unanimous verdict. After a unanimous verdict is reached, the judge is notified, and the jurors return to the court where the verdict is read by the foreman. If the verdict is guilty, the final sentencing decision rests with the judge. If the verdict is not guilty, the defendant is released.

MOTIONS

If the defendant is found guilty, the defense may move for a new trial or for a mistrial. There are several possible motions for a new trial, such as a wrong courtroom procedure, prejudice or bias on the part of witnesses, etc. If any of these motions can be proved, then a new trial will be granted.

THE SENTENCE

The sentence rests with the judge, who follows guidelines set up by the state legislature. The defendant may be sentenced to imprisonment or to a correctional institution, or he may be put on probation.

APPEALS

The defendant may appeal his case to a reviewing court by having his defense counsel prepare a brief repealing the decision of the court on the grounds of prejudice or some other injustice to him. If the defense counsel and his client are granted a new trial, it goes to the next higher court where the same procedures are utilized. An appeal case may go as high as the state supreme court, and very special cases may go as high as the United States Supreme Court. If the lower court's decision is reversed and remanded, the decision is nullified and the defendant may be tried over on the same indictment but have a different jury. If the decision is reversed, in other words, there is not sufficient evidence, the prosecuting attorney probably will not make a second attempt to convict the defendant.

CORRECTIONS

After the trial has concluded, and if the verdict of guilty has been rendered, the judge has several alternative actions to take relative to the guilty party. The two most common alternatives are sentencing to a penitentiary for a specified length of time or probation. There may be other alternatives, but these are the most common. Of course, in some situations the judge has no power to elect probation for the offender, as punishment may be specified in the state's criminal statutes.

IMPRISONMENT

The "old school" of penology advocated "lock-up" of the offender, so that he was removed from society and could do it no harm. The theory was that such punishment would discourage the individual from committing additional crimes upon release for fear of additional incarceration. Little attention was given rehabilitation or treatment, and the offender merely served his time, while his basic survival needs were met.

236

Today, the emphasis is on treatment of the offender so that he can pursue a useful life upon release. Theoretically, the prison staff will design an individualized program for each inmate that will develop his potential for rehabilitation and reintegration into the mainstream of society. This, of course, requires a staff of professional people who can analyze each individual's sociological, psychological, and medical makeup. Background information in these areas is absolutely necessary before a treatment program can be tailored to fill the individual's specific needs.

In conjunction with such treatment are the provision of additional formal and informal educational opportunities as well as social, cultural, and recreational activities. In other words, the professional staff of the prison is interested in developing a program that treats the "whole" person rather than just isolated specifics. The ultimate goal, of course, is to release a well-adjusted individual who will still maintain individual integrity.

In theory, also, prison officials are interested in keeping offenders for as short a time as possible. That is, the prisoner should be released as soon as possible after he has been rehabilitated. To incarcerate a prisoner beyond this may actually perpetuate additional problems in his treatment. It can be quite frustrating for a prisoner to know he is ready, but held back by unreasonable policy or regulations.

There are two methods by which a prisoner may be released from prison. These are the nonconditional and the conditional release. A nonconditional release may be obtained by serving the full sentence, by a court reversing its sentence, or by receiving a full pardon from the chief executive. The most common form of a conditional release is parole.

PAROLE

Parole is the process whereby the inmate is conditionally released from prison prior to serving his full sentence. This occurs when the professional prison staff determines that the person is ready to satisfactorily reintegrate into the community. Such release usually is not given until a parole board evaluates all records of the individual and agrees that he is ready for release.

The parolee is always under the supervision of a parole officer who provides necessary counseling and guidance. The parole officer also has supervisory powers and continually monitors the parolee's activities and conduct. As long as the parolee's conduct meets or excels acceptable standards during parole, he remains free. If, however, he violates the requirements of parole he may be returned to prison to serve the remainder of his sentence.

It should be realized that parole is not necessarily available to all prisoners. In many states perpetrators of serious crimes, such as murder and rape, are not eligible for parole. It should be realized also that a person may not be paroled just because he is deemed ready by the prison professional staff. Usually, the person must serve a certain portion of his sentence before he is eligible for parole. This time requirement generally runs from one-third to one-half of the sentence.

As stated earlier, parole is a conditional release. These conditions, to mention a few, may include: 1) scheduled or periodic meetings with the parole officer, 2) not fraternizing with known criminals, 3) not using alcoholic beverages, 4) not breaking any law, and 5) not leaving the jurisdiction without prior approval. These are just a few examples and conditions, which will vary among jurisdictions and according to the original crime committed.

PROBATION

Probation is the other possible alternative of the sentencing judge. This means that the person will not be sent to prison, but will remain at liberty under certain conditions prescribed by law. In granting probation the judge may, and usually does, prescribe conditions that must be met by the probationer. If the probationer does not comply with the specified conditions, his probation can be revoked and the individual incarcerated.

As in the case of parole, the conditions may vary according to the jurisdiction, the crime committed, and the age of the offender. In addition to those of parole, the probationers' conditions may include the payment of court costs or restitution to the victim.

During the probation period, the individual is usually assigned a probation officer who provides general supervision, guidance, and counseling services. The relationship with the probation officer is obviously quite important as he can, to a large degree, determine the destiny of the probationer.

The utilization of probation as an alternative to incarceration is continually becoming more widespread as correctional people recognize its value. It seems quite appropriate and beneficial not to incarcerate those people who can be rehabilitated without serving time in prison.

Of course, persons convicted of certain crimes, as determined by the state, do not have the alternative of probation available to them. Many states also restrict the use of probation to first offenders only.

Summary

The administration of justice involves the many activities of the police, judicial proceedings, and correctional agencies. What happens from the commission of a crime to the rehabilitation of the offender is referred to as the process of the administration of justice. The steps in this process are divided into four groups: 1) police process, 2) pre-trial judicial process, 3) the trial, and 4) corrections.

The police process involves the determination that a crime has been committed, the crime scene investigation, the identification of the offender, the arrest of the offender, and the booking. These may be accomplished very quickly as in the case of an on-sight arrest, but more often the process is very systematic, and involves a considerable length of time.

The pre-trial judicial process consists of a decision by the prosecutor to prosecute, the presentment, a preliminary hearing, and the arraignment. Many states use the grand jury to examine accusations of criminal charges as a preliminary to the trial. The use of the grand jury does vary from state to state.

The trial process usually involves a trial by jury even though in certain situations the judge may decide guilt or innocence on the basis of evidence presented. This second alternative is effected only when the accused waives a jury trial. The trial process can be rather lengthy, starting with the selection of a jury and concluding with either an acquittal or the sentencing of the guilty party.

The final process involves correctional personnel and agencies who are responsible for the rehabilitation of the offender. The judge may place the guilty person on probation so that he is under the supervision of a probation officer. Many people are released on parole prior to serving their entire sentence and, therefore, come under the jurisdiction of a parole officer. Prisons have many ongoing programs designed for inmates during their incarceration.

240

Discussion Questions

1. What is meant by the "administration of justice"?
2. How is justice achieved?
3. Discuss the police responsibility in the administration of justice.
4. What are the two types of arrest? Discuss legal restrictions.
5. What is the purpose of the crime scene investigation?
6. What is the police role in the trial process?
7. What is the authority and responsibility of the grand jury?
8. Under what conditions can a trial be held without a jury?
9. Discuss the trial sequence of activities.
10. Discuss the responsibility of correctional agencies and personnel in the administration of justice.

8

Government and Constitutional Rights

Since the police officer is both a representative of government and a community leader, it is important that he understand the units of government and the constitutional rights guaranteed all citizens. He certainly should know the framework within which he works, and he may have occasion to explain such divisions and rights to people with whom he comes in contact.

DIVISION OF CIVIL GOVERNMENT

The American system of government divides governmental powers and functions into three branches: 1) the legislative, 2) the executive, and 3) the judicial. The legislative branch enacts the laws, the executive branch administers and enforces them, and the judicial branch interprets the laws and judges whether persons are guilty of law violations.

The American system of government also divides governmental powers and functions into three areas: 1) the federal government, 2) the state government, and 3) the local units of government. Under the American system, every citizen in a state, for example, is a citizen of two governments: the government of the United States and of the state within which he resides.

The federal government and state government each have their own laws. Each of these governments is sovereign or supreme in the functions and powers reserved to it. The powers of the federal government are limited by the United States Constitution; state government powers are limited by the constitutions of each state. The federal government may exercise only powers that are delegated to it by the United States Constitution. The states have a reservoir of authority, in the sense that they can do anything that is not forbidden to them by the Constitution of the United States or by their own constitution.

Local government units are divisions within the state. The primary division of the state is the county. Other local government units within the state include cities, towns, and in some states boroughs and townships. These are incorporated units to which a charter has been given under authority of an act of the state legislature. The local governments have no sovereign power, but exist at the pleasure of the state government. Individuals holding office enforce the law in the manner prescribed and approved by state law. In other words, the police receive their authority from the state constitution or legislature rather than from local governmental units.

The authors of the United States Constitution set up a most complex government. Each of the three branches is independent and coordinate, and yet each is checked by the other. The judiciary hears all cases arising under the laws and the Constitution and, therefore, interprets both the fundamental law and the statute law. The federal judiciary is appointed by the President and confirmed by the Senate, and is subject to impeachment by Congress. The election of Senators for six-year terms and the appointment of federal judges assure that parts of the federal government are exposed to little direct public pressure. The lower house of Congress is more subject to such pressure. Officers of government are chosen for terms of such varying length, ranging from two years to life, that a complete change in personnel would not be possible except by a revolution.

The states are also strong, especially as they were the original sovereignties who created the United States Constitution that made the federal government. Schools, local courts, policing, the chartering of towns and cities, incorporation of banks and stock companies, the care of bridges, roads, canals, are all matters under state control.

THE LEGISLATIVE BRANCH

The legislative branch of the federal government is the Congress, composed of the Senate and House of Representatives.

246

The Congress is responsible for making laws, and also for representing the interests of state governments.

In the state, the legislative branch may be called the general assembly or the state legislature. This, too, is composed of a Senate and a House of Representatives, with the exception of Nebraska, which has a unicameral state legislature. The state legislature or general assembly enacts the laws which govern the particular state. Like the President, the governor has a veto power. This power closely associates him with the legislative branch of the state government.

Counties, being subdivisions of the state, have no legislative branch. Generally speaking, the state legislature is the legislative authority of all counties within the state.

The legislative branch of most cities is the city council. It is usually a single-chambered body, and is responsible for the enactment of city ordinances which do not fall in the classification of misdemeanors or felonies, since the state authority establishes crimes. In some cities, legislation is enacted by city managers. The legislative body of certain towns is the town meeting.

THE EXECUTIVE BRANCH

The executive branch of the United States Government carries the law into effect and applies it directly to the people. The executive branch makes most of the contacts between government and the people, and these personal contacts determine the value of government in aiding or protecting citizens. Executive officials may direct only the operations of officials and offices within the executive branch. The chief executive of the nation is the President of the United States. The administrative offices and agencies of the various federal police are under his executive authority. He is also the commander-in-chief of the armed forces.

The governor is the state's chief executive officer and the head of the law enforcement agencies of the state. In coun-

247

ties, the Board of County Commissioners is the principal executive body. Usually, law enforcement officers of the county who do not report to the courts directly or to the district attorney are under the authority of the sheriff.

THE JUDICIAL BRANCH

The judicial department interprets and applies the laws. The lower courts are independent of the higher courts, but the higher court may inject itself into the lower courts through the processes of appeal, supersedeas, habeas corpus, or other direct court orders. The federal Constitution states that the judicial branch shall be on the same level with the executive and legislative branches. The judicial power of the United States will be vested in one Supreme Court and such lower courts as Congress shall establish from time to time.

The extensive federal court system has grown from this authority. There are district courts, circuit courts of appeals, and special courts in Washington, D. C. These federal courts have jurisdiction in all cases arising under the federal Constitution, including: federal laws, admiralty law, cases where the United States is a party, cases between states, and cases between citizens of different states.

Federal courts have no jurisdiction in cases involving state affairs after they have been heard by the state supreme court. If the case has some connection with the federal Constitution, the Supreme Court decides if it has jurisdiction when a citizen appeals a state court decision or procedure.

Most states have a supreme court, a superior court, and justice courts. The district courts or superior courts are commonly called county courts because the district lines usually coincide with the county lines.

Magistrates, aldermen, and justices of the peace comprise the minor judiciary. In some respects, their powers are countywide, but their court trials are confined to the city, or jurisdiction which they represent.

248

CONSTITUTIONAL RIGHTS

Legal rights are bestowed by the federal Constitution. Police administration is directly related to constitutional rights. An important part of police training is to clarify the shadowy line between the legality and illegality of an officers's procedure.

The fundamental rights of personal freedom guaranteed citizens by the Constitution should never be infringed upon by public officials. A public official must know what the rights of the citizen are and he is duty bound to protect these rights at all times.

FREEDOM OF RELIGIOUS PRACTICE

The Constitution of the United States safeguards religious freedom by forbidding Congress to pass any law concerning "an establishment of religion." All religious expression must be kept separate from the state, and no special privileges, rights, or immunities are granted any religious body. Thus, everyone is free to worship his god or gods in his own way—or not to worship at all. Provision for protection of religious freedom is now part of all state constitutions.

FREEDOM OF SPEECH AND OF THE PRESS

Every citizen may freely speak or write on any subject, but he is responsible for what he says or what he writes.

FREEDOM OF ASSEMBLY AND THE RIGHT OF PETITION

It is very difficult for a government to enforce regulations on the right of people to assemble and discuss actions. Citizens have a right to assemble in a peaceful manner and to criticize the government, so long as they do not advocate change by unlawful means. Unlawful in this sense would usually apply to seditious or treasonable acts. The freedom of speech and the right of assembly and petition are closely bound together.

Streets and public places belong to the state or an agency of the state. Therefore, the regulation of their use for the general welfare is a responsibility of the state or its agencies. The only limitation on this power is that it be used in a reasonable, lawful, and constitutional manner.

The preservation of the public peace and order is a primary police function. The authority to investigate a breach of the peace, preserve the peace and order of the municipality, prevent an unlawful exercise of violence, and compel citizens to abstain from riot, rout, and unlawful assembly, is regarded as an inherent municipal power essential to municipal life.

FREEDOM FROM UNREASONABLE SEARCH AND SEIZURE

The right of the people to be secure in their persons, houses, papers, and effects, against unreasonable search and seizure shall not be violated, and no warrant shall be issued, but upon probable cause, supported by oath or affirmation, in particular describing the place to be searched, and the persons or things to be seized.

It is not a violation of this clause for an officer making an arrest, with or without a warrant, to discover and seize any evidence found on the prisoner or the premises in his immediate vicinity if it is directly connected with the offense charged.

FREEDOM FROM DEPRIVATION WITHOUT DUE PROCESS OF LAW

In no criminal prosecution can the accused be deprived of his life, liberty, or property unless by the judgment of his equals or the law of the land. The key to correct legal functions is found in the phrase *due process of law*—an orderly, recognized legal procedure enforced, and within jurisdictional limits.

FREEDOM FROM SELF-INCRIMINATION

An accused person is always innocent until the court renders a verdict of guilty, and only then may he be punished. In no criminal prosecutions can the accused be compelled to give evidence against himself. There is no legal way of forcing him to talk except in a court trial, but a court can order a witness to talk under certain restrictions or the witness may be punished for disobedience.

FREEDOM FROM UNKNOWN AND UNSEEN ACCUSERS AND ACCUSATIONS

In all criminal prosecutions, the accused has a right to demand the nature and cause of the accusation against him and to meet the witness face to face. Witnesses meet face to face in a court hearing. This clause forms the basis for requiring a signed complaint in connection with arrest. In all criminal cases, the witness must be examined in the presence of the accused and be subject to cross-examination.

RIGHT TO BAIL AND THE USE OF WRIT OF HABEAS CORPUS

All prisoners shall be bailable by sufficient security except for capital offenses where the proof is evident or presumption of guilt great. The privilege of the writ of habeas corpus shall not be suspended unless the public safety may require it in a case of rebellion or invasion. Bail is the delivery of the accused to others upon their giving, with himself, sufficient security for his appearance when called. It also means that those persons agree to produce the accused when called upon to do so or to forfeit the security. Such security is properly called the bail bond. There is some serious consideration for revising statutes and legislation relative to the use of bail bonds.

Habeas corpus is a writ or an order to the person detaining another, commanding him to produce the prisoner at a certain time and place, with the day and the cause of his arrest detention indicated, in order to comply with whatever the judge who awarded the writ shall consider proper. The true use of the writ is to insure a legal inquiry in to the cause of imprisonment, and to produce the release of the prisoner if his imprisonment is found illegal.

RIGHT TO A SPEEDY TRIAL BY AN IMPARTIAL JURY

Basically, this means that in all criminal prosecutions the accused has the right to a speedy, public trial by an impartial jury of the vicinity, whether the prosecution be by indictment or by information. Jury of the vicinity does not require trial in the county where the crime was actually committed, as there is an allowance for change in venue. There may be instances where neither the prosecution nor the defense can expect a fair trial in the local county and, therefore, they agree that a change of venue would be important if justice is to be achieved.

FREEDOM FROM EXCESSIVE BAIL AND FINES AND FROM CRUEL AND UNUSUAL PUNISHMENT

Excessive bail shall not be required, nor excessive fines imposed, nor cruel punishment inflicted, the judiciary having the responsibility of setting the bail and assessing the fines and other punishments. An accused person is innocent until a verdict of guilty is pronounced by the court; therefore, punishment is a function reserved to the judicial branch, and must not be inflicted until after the accused has been found guilty, and the law has affixed a certain punishment. Police or accusers have no right to inflict any kind of punishment on the accused before he is convicted. The American system of law presumes a man to be innocent until he is proven guilty. This presumption attends all proceedings against the defendant from their initiation until their resolution in a verdict which either finds the party guilty, or converts the presumption of innocence into a fact.

DOUBLE JEOPARDY

A person is protected by the Constitution of the United States from being tried for the same crime twice. When a person has been tried in court and found innocent, he cannot again be tried for that same offense.

Summary

The government of the United States is divided into three branches: 1) the legislative, 2) the executive, and 3) the judicial. The legislative branch enacts law, the executive branch administers and enforces law, and the judicial branch interprets law. The American system of government also divides government powers and functions into three levels: 1) federal, 2) state, and 3) local.

The powers of the federal and state governments are limited by their respective constitutions. The federal government may exercise only powers that are delegated to it by the United States Constitution. All powers not delegated to the federal government by the Constitution are reserved to the states. By virtue of this, the states have a reservoir of authority, in the sense that they can do anything which is not forbidden to them by the Constitution of the United States or by their own constitution. Each state, therefore, has the authority to establish state and local police agencies.

The Constitution of the United States guarantees certain fundamental rights to all citizens that cannot be denied them. It is in these fundamental rights of personal freedom that many of the rights, duties, and obligations of the police and courts are found. Public officials must guarantee these rights, and should not be in a position to be accused of infringing upon them.

Discussion Questions

1. Why should police officers be familiar with the organization of government?
2. What are three branches of the federal government?
3. Explain the function of each branch of the federal government.
4. What relationship exists between the branches of the federal government?
5. From what source do local and state police derive their authority?
6. What level of government has the primary police authority?
7. Discuss the various levels of government as they relate to the police function.
8. What is the police responsibility in guaranteeing fundamental rights to citizens?
9. How does the guarantee of freedom from unreasonable search and seizure affect the police function?
10. What is "due process of law"?

Bibliography

Adam, Hargrave L. *The Police Encyclopedia*, vol. 1. Waverly Book Company, Ltd., 1925.

Brown, Douglas G. *The Rise of Scotland Yard*. New York: G. P. Putnam's Sons.

Cross, Wilbur L. *The History of Henry Fielding*, vol. 1. New York: Russell & Russell, Inc., 1963.

Feiling, Keith. *A History of England*. London: Macmillan and Co., Ltd., 1963.

Fosdick, Raymond B. *American Police Systems*. New York: The Century Company, 1920.

Mays, Katherine. *Justice To All: The Story of the Pennsylvania State Police*. New York and London: G. P. Putnam's Sons, The Knickerbocker Press, 1917.

Morrell, W. P. *British Colonial Policy in the Age of Peel and Russell*. New York: Barnes and Noble, Inc., 1930.

Rowell, Henry Thompson. *Rome in the Augustan Age*. Norman: University of Oklahoma Press, 1962.

Wells, J., and Barrow, R. H. *A Short History of the Roman Empire*. New York: Barnes and Noble, Inc., 1958.

Appendixes

LEGAL PHRASES AND DEFINITIONS

The following legal terms and words frequently arise in police work, and all students should be familiar with their meaning. The definitions listed are clear and as devoid of legal phraseology as is consistent with accuracy. It must be realized, however, that some definitions will vary from state to state. The definitions are, therefore, given in rather general terms. Where questions arise, the student should consult his state's criminal code.

Accessory before the fact.   One who helps another to commit a crime, though he is absent when the crime actually is committed.

Accessory after the fact.   One who harbors, assists, or protects another person when he knows that person has committed a crime.

Accomplice.   One who is directly concerned in the commission of a crime with another person, or persons, whether he actually commits the crime or abets others. The term *principal* means the same thing, except that one may be a principal if he commits a crime without being aided by others.

Acquit.   To legally free a person from an accusation of criminal guilt.

Adjournment.   Termination or postponement of a session or hearing to some other time or place.

Adult.   Any person who is twenty-one years of age or older.

Adultery.   Voluntary sexual intercourse where one or both of the participants is married, but not to each other. Prosecution usually is commenced only on complaint of spouse.

Affidavit.   A voluntary written or printed declaration or statement of facts confirmed by the oath or affirmation of the person making it, taken before an officer having the authority to administer such oath.

Affirmation.   An oath which means that one calls upon God to witness the truth of what he says. So we generally swear on the *Bible*. However, some people, because of their religious beliefs or their lack of religion, refuse to swear in such a manner. Such people are allowed to swear on their conscience that what they say is true. This may be called an *affirmation* or an *asseveration*. It has the same legal force and effect as an oath.

Alias. Any name by which a person is known other than his true name.

Alibi. A claim that one was in a place different from that claimed.

Appeal. A case carried to a higher court, in which it is asked that the decision of the lower court, in which the case originated, be altered or overruled completely.

Arraign. When a person is arrested and brought before a court, the complaint is read to him and he pleads guilty or not guilty to the charge.

Arrest. To take a person into custody so that he may be held to answer for a crime.

Arson. The willful or malicious setting afire of a building with the intent to defraud.

Asportation. The moving of an object from its original position.

Assault. An unlawful attempt to hurt another person physically. If the person is actually beaten, the additional act is called *battery*.

Bail. To release a person from jail by guaranteeing that he shall remain within the jurisdiction and call of the court.

Battery. Wrongful physical force inflicted on another without his consent. It is associated with an assault, which is the attempt to inflict the force. If the attempt is completed, the result is a battery.

Blackmail. To extort something of value from another by the threat of accusation or exposure.

Brief. A summary of the law relating to a case, which is prepared by the attorneys for both parties to a case, and given to the judge.

Burden of proof. The burden of proving the fact in issue. The prosecution must prove beyond a reasonable doubt that the defendant is guilty.

Burglary. Breaking into another person's house or other building with the intention of committing a felony or stealing something of value. The laws relative to burglary vary from state to state.

Capital crime. Any crime punishable by death.

Coercion. Compelling a person to do that which he does not have to do, or to omit what he may legally do, by an illegal threat, force, intimidation, etc.

Complaint. A sworn written allegation that a specified person committed a crime. It is the complaint that gives the court jurisdiction to try the case.

Conspiracy. A combination of two or more persons for the purpose of committing a crime.

Corporeal. Relating to the body. Thus, corporeal punishment is force used against the body of another.

Corpus delicti. The body or essence of a crime; all things necessary to constitute a crime.

Defraud. To withhold from another what is justly due him, or to deprive him of a right by artifice or deception.

Defendant. The party against whom an action at law or in equity is brought.

Deposition. The written testimony of a witness given under oath.

Domicile. The place where a person has his permanent residence.

Duress. To influence by force or by imparting fear of injury.

Embezzlement. Misappropriating the personal property of another person who has given one the property for a specified purpose.

Eminent domain. The power of the state, or a political subdivision, to acquire private property for public use through appraisal, court action, and payment of a fair price.

Evidence. All the means used to prove or disprove a fact and issue.

261

Extortion. The obtaining of property from another with his consent induced by wrongful use of force or fear, or under color of official right.

Extradition. The surrender of a fugitive from justice from one nation to another. A similar surrender between states is known technically as *rendition*, although by common usage, both types are called extradition.

Felony. An offense punishable by death or by imprisonment in a state prison.

Fence. A term applied to a professional receiver of stolen goods.

Grand jury. A jury of inquiry who is summoned and returned by the sheriff to each session of the criminal courts, and whose duty it is to receive complaints and accusations in criminal cases, hear the evidence adduced on the part of the state, and file bills of indictment in cases where they are satisfied a trial ought to be held. They are first sworn, and instructed by the court. This is called a grand jury because it comprises a greater number of jurors than the ordinary trial jury or petit jury.

Homicide. Killing of one human being by another.

Indict. To accuse of crime, in writing, by a grand jury. The indictment gives a court jurisdiction to try the case.

Injunction. An order by a court prohibiting a defendant from committing an act which is injurious to the plaintiff.

Intent. A design or determination of the mind to do or not to do a certain thing. Criminal intent is the intent to break the law. Intent usually is determined by the nature of one's act.

Justifiable homicide. The excused killing of a human being by accident, in performance of a legal duty, in self-defense, in defense of one's home or family, etc.

Larceny. Unlawful taking of property belonging to another.

Manslaughter. The unlawful killing without malice of another.

Misdemeanor. An indictable offense not amounting to a felony.

Modus operandi. Method of operation by criminals.

262

Parole. A conditional release from prison.

Perjury. The act of willfully swearing falsely.

Petit jury. The ordinary jury of twelve men for the trial of a civil or criminal action. So called to distinguish it from the grand jury, a petit jury is a body of twelve men impanelled and sworn to try and determine, by true and unanimous verdict, any questions or issues of fact, in any civil or criminal action or proceeding according to law and the evidence given them in the court.

Plaintiff. In a criminal case, the complainant.

Postmortem. Meaning after death. Commonly applied to examinations of a dead body. An *autopsy* is a postmortem examination to determine the cause of death.

Preliminary hearing. A hearing before a magistrate to decide if there is sufficient evidence to hold the defendant for further action.

Probation. The type of penalty whereby a convicted person is put under the jurisdiction of probation officers for a stated time, instead of being sent to prison.

Sentence. The judgment formally pronounced by the court or judge upon the defendant after his conviction in a criminal prosecution, awarding the punishment to be inflicted. In civil cases, the terms *judgment, decision, award, finding*, etc., are used.

Subpoena. A written order to appear at a trial as a witness.

Summons. A signed request directing a person to appear in court at a specified time to explain a charge made against him.

Venue. A neighborhood; the neighbhood, place, or county in which an injury is declared to have been done.

Verdict. The decision of a jury.

Warrant. A writ issued by a court or magistrate ordering a peace officer to arrest the one named therein for a crime.

The Constitution of the United States of America

We the people of the United States, in order to form a more perfect union, establish justice, insure domestic tranquility, provide for the common defense, promote the general welfare, and secure the blessings of liberty to ourselves and our posterity, do ordain and establish this Constitution for the United States of America.

ARTICLE I

Section 1. All legislative powers herein granted shall be vested in a Congress of the United States, which shall consist of a Senate and House of Representatives.

Section 2. 1. The House of Representatives shall be composed of members chosen every second year by the people of the several States, and the electors in each State shall have the qualifications requisite for electors of the most numerous branch of the State legislature.

2. No person shall be a representative who shall not have attained to the age of twenty-five years, and been seven years a citizen of the United States, and who shall not, when elected, be an inhabitant of that State in which he shall be chosen.

3. Representatives and direct taxes[1] shall be apportioned among the several States which may be included within this Union, according to their respective numbers, which shall be determined by adding to the whole number of free persons, including those bound to service for a term of years, and excluding Indians not taxed, three fifths of all other persons.[2] The actual enumeration shall by made within three years after the first meeting of the Congress of the United States, and within every subsequent term of ten years, in such manner as they shall by law direct. The number of representatives shall not exceed one for every thirty thousand, but each State shall have at least one representative; and until such enumeration shall be made, the State of New Hampshire shall be entitled to choose three, Massachusetts eight, Rhode Island and Providence Plantations one, Connecticut five, New York six, New Jersey four, Pennsylvania eight, Delaware one, Maryland six, Virginia ten, North Carolina five, South Carolina five, and Georgia three.

4. When vacancies happen in the representation from any State, the executive authority thereof shall issue writs of election to fill such vacancies.

5. The House of Representatives shall choose their speaker and other officers; and shall have the sole power of impeachment.

Section 3. 1. The Senate of the United States shall be composed of two senators from each State, chosen by the legislature thereof,[3] for six years; and each senator shall have one vote.

2. Immediately after they shall be assembled in consequence of the first election, they shall be divided as equally as may be into three classes. The seats of the senators of the first class shall be vacated at the expiration of the second year, of the second class at the expiration of the fourth year and of the third class at the expiration of the sixth year, so that one third may be chosen every second year; and if vacancies happen by resignation, or otherwise, during the recess of the legislature of any State, the executive thereof may make temporary appointments until the next meeting of the legislature, which shall then fill such vacancies.[4]

3. No person shall be a senator who shall not have attained to the age of thirty years, and been nine years a citizen of the United States, and who shall not, when elected, be an inhabitant of that State for which he shall be chosen.

4. The Vice President of the United States shall be President of the Senate, but shall have no vote, unless they be equally divided.

5. The Senate shall choose their other officers, and also a president pro tempore, in the absence of the Vice President, or when he shall exercise the office of the President of the United States.

6. The Senate shall have the sole power to try all impeachments. When sitting for that purpose, they shall be on oath or affirmation. When the President of the United States is tried, the chief justice shall preside: and no person shall be convicted without the concurrence of two thirds of the members present.

7. Judgment in cases of impeachment shall not extend further than to removal from office, and disqualifications to hold and enjoy any office of honor, trust or profit under the United States: but the party convicted shall nevertheless be liable and subject to indictment, trial, judgment and punishment, according to law.

Section 4. 1. The times, places, and manner of holding elections for senators and representatives, shall be prescribed in each State by the legislature thereof: but the Congress may at any time by law make or alter such regulations, except as to the places of choosing senators.

2. The Congress shall assemble at least once in every year, and such meeting shall be on the first Monday in December, unless they shall by law appoint a different day.

Section 5. 1. Each House shall be the judge of the elections, returns and qualifications of its own members, and a majority of each shall constitute a quorum to do business; but a smaller number may adjourn from day to day, and may be authorized to compel the attendance of absent members, in such manner, and under such penalties as each House may provide.

[1] Altered by the 16th Amendment.
[2] Altered by the 14th Amendment.
[3] Superseded by the 17th Amendment.

[4] Altered by the 17th Amendment.

2. Each House may determine the rules of its proceedings, punish its members for disorderly behavior, and, with the concurrence of two thirds, expel a member.

3. Each House shall keep a journal of its proceedings, and from time to time publish the same, excepting such parts as may in their judgment require secrecy; and the yeas and nays of the members of either House on any question shall, at the desire of one fifth of those present, be entered on the journal.

4. Neither House, during the session of Congress, shall, without the consent of the other, adjourn for more than three days, nor to any other place than that in which the two Houses shall be sitting.

Section 6. 1. The senators and representatives shall receive a compensation for their services, to be ascertained by law, and paid out of the Treasury of the United States. They shall in all cases, except treason, felony, and breach of the peace, be privileged from arrest during their attendance at the session of their respective Houses, and in going to and returning from the same; and for any speech or debate in either House, they shall not be questioned in any other place.

2. No senator or representative shall, during the time for which he was elected, be appointed to any civil office under the authority of the United States, which shall have been created, or the emoluments whereof shall have been increased, during such time; and no person holding any office under the United States shall be a member of either House during his continuance in office.

Section 7. 1. All bills for raising revenue shall originate in the House of Representatives; but the Senate may propose or concur with amendments as on other bills.

2. Every bill which shall have passed the House of Representatives and the Senate, shall, before it become a law, be presented to the President of the United States; If he approves he shall sign it, but if not he shall return it, with his objections, to that House in which it shall have originated, who shall enter the objections at large on their journal, and proceed to reconsider it. If after such reconsideration two thirds of that House shall agree to pass the bill, it shall be sent, together with the objections, to the other House, by which it shall likewise be reconsidered, and if approved by two thirds of that House, it shall become a law. But in all such cases the votes of both Houses shall be determined by yeas and nays, and the names of the persons voting for and against the bill shall be entered on the journal of each House respectively. If any bill shall not be returned by the President within ten days (Sundays excepted) after it shall have been presented to him, the same shall be a law, in like manner as if he had signed it, unless the Congress by their adjournment prevent its return, in which case it shall not be a law.

3. Every order, resolution, or vote to which the concurrence of the Senate and the House of Representatives may be necessary (except on a question of adjournment) shall be presented to the President of the United States; and before the same shall take effect, shall be approved by him, or being disapproved by him, shall be repassed by two thirds of the Senate and House of Representatives, according to the rules and limitations prescribed in the case of a bill.

Section 8. The Congress shall have the power

1. To lay and collect taxes, duties, imposts, and excises, to pay the debts and provide for the common defense and general welfare of the United States; but all duties, imposts, and excises shall be uniform throughout the United States;

2. To borrow money on the credit of the United States;

3. To regulate commerce with foreign nations, and among the several States, and with the Indian tribes;

4. To establish an uniform rule of naturalization, and uniform laws on the subject of bankruptcies throughout the United States;

5. To coin money, regulate the value thereof, and of foreign coin, and fix the standard of weights and measures;

6. To provide for the punishment of counterfeiting the securities and current coin of the United States;

7. To establish post offices and post roads;

8. To promote the progress of science and useful arts, by securing for limited times to authors and inventors the exclusive right to their respective writings and discoveries;

9. To constitute tribunals inferior to the Supreme Court;

10. To define and punish piracies and felonies committed on the high seas, and offenses against the law of nations;

11. To declare war, grant letters of marque and reprisal, and make rules concerning captures on land and water;

12. To raise and support armies, but no appropriation of money to that use shall be for a longer term than two years;

13. To provide and maintain a navy;

14. To make rules for the government and regulation of the land and naval forces;

15. To provide for calling forth the militia to execute the laws of the Union, suppress insurrections and repel invasions;

16. To provide for organizing, arming, and disciplining the militia, and for governing such part of them as may be employed in the service of the United States, reserving to the States respectively, the appointment of the officers, and the authority of training the militia according to the discipline prescribed by Congress;

17. To exercise exclusive legislation in all cases whatsoever, over such district (not exceeding ten miles square) as may, by cession of particular States, and the acceptance of Congress, become the seat of the government of the United States, and to exercise like authority over all places purchased by the consent of the legislature of the State in which the same shall be, for the erection of forts, magazines, arsenals, dockyards, and other needful buildings; and

18. To make all laws which shall be necessary and proper for carrying into execution the foregoing powers, and all other powers vested by this Constitution in the government of the United States, or any department or officer thereof.

Section 9. 1. The migration or importation of such persons as any of the States now existing shall think proper to admit, shall not be prohibited by the Congress prior to the year one thousand eight hundred and eight, but a tax or duty may be imposed on such importation, not exceeding ten dollars for each person.

2. The privilege of the writ of habeas corpus shall not be suspended, unless when in cases of rebellion or invasion the public safety may require it.

3. No bill of attainder or ex post facto law shall be passed.

4. No capitation, or other direct, tax shall be laid, unless in proportion to the census or enumeration hereinbefore directed to be taken.[5]

5. No tax or duty shall be laid on articles exported from any State.

6. No preference shall be given by any regulation of commerce or revenue to the ports of one State over those of another: nor shall vessels bound to, or from, one State be obliged to enter, clear, or pay duties in another.

7. No money shall be drawn from the treasury, but in consequence of appropriations made by law; and a regular statement and account of the receipts and expenditures of all public money shall be published from time to time.

8. No title of nobility shall be granted by the United States: and no person holding any office of profit or trust under them, shall, without the consent of the Congress, accept of any present, emolument, office, or title, of any kind whatever, from any king, prince, or foreign State.

Section 10. 1. No State shall enter into any treaty, alliance, or confederation; grant letters of marque and reprisal; coin money; emit bills of credit; make any thing but gold and silver coin a tender in payment of debts; pass any bill of attainder, ex post facto law, or law impairing the obligation of contracts, or grant any title of nobility.

2. No State shall, without the consent of the Congress, lay any imposts or duties on imports or exports, except what may be absolutely necessary for executing its inspection laws: and the net produce of all duties and imposts laid by any State on imports or exports, shall be for the use of the treasury of the United States; and all such laws shall be subject to the revision and control of the Congress.

3. No State shall, without the consent of the Congress, lay any duty of tonnage, keep troops, or ships of war in time of peace, enter into any agreement or compact with another State, or with a foreign power, or engage in war, unless actually invaded, or in such imminent danger as will not admit of delay.

ARTICLE II

Section 1. 1. The executive power shall be vested in a President of the United States of America. He shall hold his office during the term of four years, and, together with the Vice President, chosen for the same term, be elected, as follows:

2. Each State shall appoint, in such manner as the legislature thereof may direct, a number of electors, equal to the whole number of senators and representatives to which the State may be entitled in the Congress: but no senator or representative, or person holding an office of

trust or profit under the United States, shall be appointed an elector.

The electors shall meet in their respective States, and vote by ballot for two persons, of whom one at least shall not be an inhabitant of the same State with themselves. And they shall make a list of all the persons voted for, and of the number of votes for each; which list they shall sign and certify, and transmit sealed to the seat of the government of the United States, directed to the president of the Senate. The president of the Senate shall, in the presence of the Senate and House of Representatives, open all the certificates, and the votes shall then be counted. The person having the greatest number of votes shall be the President, if such number be a majority of the whole number of electors appointed; and if there be more than one who have such majority, and have an equal number of votes, then the House of Representatives shall immediately choose by ballot one of them for President; and if no person have a majority, then from the five highest on the list the said House shall in like manner choose the President. But in choosing the President, the votes shall be taken by States, the representation from each State having one vote; a quorum for this purpose shall consist of a member or members from two thirds of the States, and a majority of all the States shall be necessary to a choice. In every case, after the choice of the President, the person having the greatest number of votes of the electors shall be the Vice President. But if there should remain two or more who have equal votes, the Senate shall choose from them by ballot the Vice President.[6]

3. The Congress may determine the time of choosing the electors, and the day on which they shall give their votes; which day shall be the same throughout the United States.

4. No person except a natural born citizen, or a citizen of the United States, at the time of the adoption of this Constitution, shall be eligible to the office of President; neither shall any person be eligible to that office who shall not have attained to the age of thirty-five years, and been fourteen years a resident within the United States.

5. In case of the removal of the President from office, or of his death, resignation, or inability to discharge the powers and duties of the said office, the same shall devolve on the Vice President, and the Congress may by law provide for the case of removal, death, resignation or inability, both of the President and Vice President, declaring what officer shall then act as President, and such officer shall act accordingly, until the disability be removed, or a President shall be elected.

6. The President shall, at stated times, receive for his services a compensation, which shall neither be increased nor diminished during the period for which he shall have been elected, and he shall not receive within that period any other emolument from the United States, or any of them.

7. Before he enter on the execution of his office, he shall take the following oath or affirmation:—"I do solemnly swear (or affirm) that I will faithfully execute the office of President of the United States, and will to the best of my

[5] Superseded by the 16th Amendment.

[6] Superseded by the 12th Amendment.

ability, preserve, protect, and defend the Constitution of the United States."

Section 2. 1. The President shall be commander in chief of the army and navy of the United States, and of the militia of the several States, when called into the actual service of the United States; he may require the opinion, in writing, of the principal officer in each of the executive departments, upon any subject relating to the duties of their respective offices, and he shall have power to grant reprieves and pardons for offenses against the United States, except in cases of impeachment.

2. He shall have power, by and with the advice and consent of the Senate, to make treaties, provided two thirds of the senators present concur; and he shall nominate, and by and with the advice and consent of the Senate, shall appoint ambassadors, other public ministers and consuls, judges of the Supreme Court, and all other officers of the United States, whose appointments are not herein otherwise provided for, and which shall be established by law: but the Congress may by law vest the appointment of such inferior officers, as they think proper, in the President alone, in the courts of law, or in the heads of departments.

3. The President shall have power to fill up all vacancies that may happen during the recess of the Senate, by granting commissions which shall expire at the end of their next session.

Section 3. He shall from time to time give to the Congress information of the state of the Union, and recommend to their consideration such measures as he shall judge necessary and expedient; he may, on extraordinary occasions, convene both Houses, or either of them, and in case of disagreement between them with respect to the time of adjournment, he may adjourn them to such time as he shall think proper; he shall receive ambassadors and other public ministers; he shall take care that the laws be faithfully executed, and shall commission all the officers of the United States.

Section 4. The President, Vice President, and all civil officers of the United States, shall be removed from office on impeachment for, and conviction of, treason, bribery, or other high crimes and misdemeanors.

ARTICLE III

Section 1. The judicial power of the United States shall be vested in one Supreme Court, and in such inferior courts as the Congress may from time to time ordain and establish. The judges, both of the Supreme and inferior courts, shall hold their offices during good behavior, and shall, at stated times, receive for their services, a compensation, which shall not be diminished during their continuance in office.

Section 2. 1. The judicial power shall extend to all cases, in law and equity, arising under this Constitution, the laws of the United States, and treaties made, or which shall be made, under their authority;—to all cases affecting ambassadors, other public ministers and consuls;—to all cases of admiralty and maritime jurisdiction;—to controversies to which the United States shall be a party;[7]—to controversies between two or more

[7] Cf. the 11th Amendment.

States;—between a State and citizens of another State;—between citizens of different States;—between citizens of the same State claiming lands under grants of different States, and between a State, or the citizens thereof, and foreign States, citizens or subjects.

2. In all cases affecting ambassadors, other public ministers and consuls, and those in which a State shall be party, the Supreme Court shall have original jurisdiction. In all the other cases before mentioned, the Supreme Court shall have appellate jurisdiction, both as to law and fact, with such exceptions, and under such regulations as the Congress shall make.

3. The trial of all crimes, except in cases of impeachment, shall be by jury; and such trial shall be held in the State where the said crimes shall have been committed; but when not committed within any State, the trial shall be at such place or places as the Congress may by law have directed.

Section 3. 1. Treason against the United States shall consist only in levying war against them, or in adhering to their enemies, giving them aid and comfort. No person shall be convicted of treason unless on the testimony of two witnesses to the same overt act, or on confession in open court.

2. The Congress shall have power to declare the punishment of treason, but no attainder of treason shall work corruption of blood, or forfeiture except during the life of the person attainted.

ARTICLE IV

Section 1. Full faith and credit shall be given in each State to the public acts, records, and judicial proceedings of every other State. And the Congress may by general laws prescribe the manner in which such acts, records and proceedings shall be proved, and the effect thereof.

Section 2. 1. The citizens of each State shall be entitled to all privileges and immunities of citizens in the several States.[8]

2. A person charged in any State with treason, felony, or other crime, who shall flee from justice, and be found in another State, shall on demand of the executive authority of the State from which he fled, be delivered up to be removed to the State having jurisdiction of the crime.

3. No person held to service or labor in one State under the laws thereof, escaping into another, shall, in consequence of any law or regulation therein, be discharged from such service or labor, but shall be delivered up on claim of the party to whom such service or labor may be due.[9]

Section 3. 1. New States may be admitted by the Congress into this Union; but no new State shall be formed or erected within the jurisdiction of any other State; nor any State be formed by the junction of two or more States, or parts of States, without the consent of the legislatures of the States concerned as well as of the Congress.

2. The Congress shall have power to dispose of and make all needful rules and regulations respecting the

[8] Superseded by the 14th Amendment, Sec. 1.
[9] Voided by the 13th Amendment.

territory or other property belonging to the United States; and nothing in this Constitution shall be so construed as to prejudice any claims of the United States, or of any particular State.

Section 4. The United States shall guarantee to every State in this Union a republican form of government, and shall protect each of them against invasion; and on application of the legislature, or of the executive (when the legislature cannot be convened) against domestic violence.

ARTICLE V

The Congress, whenever two thirds of both Houses shall deem it necessary, shall propose amendments to this Constitution, or, on the application of the legislatures of two thirds of the several States, shall call a convention for proposing amendments, which in either case, shall be valid to all intents and purposes, as part of this Constitution, when ratified by the legislatures of three fourths of the several States, or by conventions in three fourths thereof, as the one or the other mode of ratification may be proposed by the Congress; Provided that no amendment which may be made prior to the year one thousand eight hundred and eight shall in any manner affect the first and fourth clauses in the ninth section of the first article; and that no State, without its consent, shall be deprived of its equal suffrage in the Senate.

ARTICLE VI

1. All debts contracted and engagements entered into, before the adoption of this Constitution, shall be as valid against the United States under this Constitution, as under the Confederation.

2. This Constitution, and the laws of the United States which shall be made in pursuance thereof; and all treaties made, or which shall be made, under the authority of the United States, shall be the supreme law of the land; and the Judges in every State shall be bound thereby, any thing in the Constitution or laws of any State to the contrary notwithstanding.

3. The senators and representatives before mentioned, and the members of the several State legislatures, and all executive and judicial officers, both of the United States and of the several States, shall be bound by oath or affirmation to support this Constitution; but no religious test shall ever be required as a qualification to any office or public trust under the United States.

ARTICLE VII

The ratification of the conventions of nine States shall be sufficient for the establishment of this Constitution between the States so ratifying the same.

Done in Convention by the unanimous consent of the States present the seventeenth day of September in the year of our Lord one thousand seven hundred and eighty-seven, and of the independence of the United States of America the twelfth. In witness whereof we have hereunto subscribed our names.

[Names omitted]

* * *

Articles in addition to, and amendment of, the Constitution of the United States of America, proposed by Congress, and ratified by the legislatures of the several States, pursuant to the fifth article of the original Constitution.

AMENDMENT I [First ten amendments ratified December 15, 1791]

Congress shall make no law respecting an establishment of religion, or prohibiting the free exercise thereof; or abridging the freedom of speech, or of the press; or the right of the people peaceably to assemble, and to petition the government for a redress of grievances.

AMENDMENT II

A well regulated militia, being necessary to the security of a free State, the right of the people to keep and bear arms, shall not be infringed.

AMENDMENT III

No soldier shall, in time of peace be quartered in any house, without the consent of the owner, nor in time of war, but in a manner to be prescribed by law.

AMENDMENT IV

The right of the people to secure in their persons, houses, papers, and effects, against unreasonable searches and seizures, shall not be violated, and no warrants shall issue, but upon probable cause, supported by oath or affirmation, and particularly describing the place to be searched, and the persons or things to be seized.

AMENDMENT V

No person shall be held to answer for a capital, or otherwise infamous crime, unless on a presentment or indictment of a grand jury, except in cases arising in the land or naval forces, or in the militia, when in actual service in time of war or public danger; nor shall any person be subject for the same offense to be twice put in jeopardy of life or limb; nor shall be compelled in any criminal case to be a witness against himself, nor be deprived of life, liberty, or property, without due process of law; nor shall private property be taken for public use, without just compensation.

AMENDMENT VI

In all criminal prosecutions, the accused shall enjoy the right to a speedy and public trial, by an impartial jury of the State and district wherein the crime shall have been committed, which district shall have been previously ascertained by law, and to be informed of the nature and cause of the accusation; to be confronted with the witnesses against him; to have compulsory process for obtaining witnesses in his favor, and to have the assistance of counsel for his defense.

AMENDMENT VII

In suits at common law, where the value in controversy shall exceed twenty dollars, the right of trial by jury shall be preserved, and no fact tried by a jury shall be otherwise reëxamined in any court of the United States, than according to the rules of the common law.

AMENDMENT VIII

Excessive bail shall not be required, nor excessive fines imposed, nor cruel and unusual punishments inflicted.

AMENDMENT IX

The enumeration in the Constitution of certain rights shall not be construed to deny or disparage others retained by the people.

AMENDMENT X

The powers not delegated to the United States by the Constitution, nor prohibited by it to the States, are reserved to the States respectively, or to the people.

AMENDMENT XI [Ratified January 8, 1798]

The judicial power of the United States shall not be construed to extend to any suit in law or equity, commenced or prosecuted against one of the United States by citizens of another State, or by citizens or subjects of any foreign State.

AMENDMENT XII [Ratified September 25, 1804]

The electors shall meet in their respective States, and vote by ballot for President and Vice President, one of whom, at least, shall not be an inhabitant of the same State with themselves; they shall name in their ballots the person voted for as President, and in distinct ballots, the person voted for as Vice President, and they shall make distinct lists of all persons voted for as President and of all persons voted for as Vice President, and of the number of votes for each, which lists they shall sign and certify, and transmit sealed to the seat of the government of the United States, directed to the President of the Senate;—The President of the Senate shall, in the presence of the Senate and House of Representatives, open all the certificates and the votes shall then be counted;—The person having the greatest number of votes for President, shall be the President, if such number be a majority of the whole number of electors appointed; and if no person have such majority, then from the persons having the highest numbers not exceeding three on the list of those voted for as President, the House of Representatives shall choose immediately, by ballot, the President. But in choosing the President, the votes shall be taken by States, the representation from each State having one vote; a quorum for this purpose shall consist of a member or members from two thirds of the States, and a majority of all the States shall be necessary to a choice. And if the House of Representatives shall not choose a President whenever the right of choice shall devolve upon them, before the fourth day of March next following, then the Vice President shall act as President, as in the case of the death or other constitutional disability of the President. The person having the greatest number of votes as Vice President shall be the Vice President, if such number be a majority of the whole number of electors appointed, and if no person have a majority, then from the two highest numbers on the list, the Senate shall choose the Vice President; a quorum for the purpose shall consist of two thirds of the whole number of Senators, and a majority of the whole number shall be necessary to a choice. But no person constitutionally ineligible to the office of President shall be eligible to that of Vice President of the United States.

AMENDMENT XIII [Ratified December 18, 1865]

Section 1. Neither slavery nor involuntary servitude, except as a punishment for crime whereof the party shall have been duly convicted, shall exist within the United States, or any place subject to their jurisdiction.

Section 2. Congress shall have power to enforce this article by appropriate legislation.

AMENDMENT XIV [Ratified July 28, 1868]

Section 1. All persons born or naturalized in the United States, and subject to the jurisdiction thereof, are citizens of the United States and of the State wherein they reside. No State shall make or enforce any law which shall abridge the privileges or immunities of citizens of the United States; nor shall any State deprive any person of life, liberty, or property, without due process of law; nor deny to any person within its jurisdiction the equal protection of the laws.

Section 2. Representatives shall be apportioned among the several States according to their respective numbers, counting the whole number of persons in each State, excluding Indians not taxed. But when the right to vote at any election for the choice of electors for President and Vice President of the United States, representatives in Congress, the executive and judicial officers of a State, or the members of the legislature thereof, is denied to any of the male inhabitants of such State, being twenty-one years of age, and citizens of the United States, or in any way abridged, except for participating in rebellion, or other crime, the basis of representation therein shall be reduced in the proportion which the number of such male citizens shall bear to the whole number of male citizens twenty-one years of age in such State.

Section 3. No person shall be a senator or representative in Congress, or elector of President and Vice President, or hold any office, civil or military, under the United States, or under any State, who having previously taken an oath, as a member of Congress, or as an officer of the United States, or as a member of any State legislature, or as an executive or judicial officer of any State, to support the Constitution of the United States, shall have engaged in insurrection or rebellion against the same, or given aid or comfort to the enemies thereof. But Congress may by a vote of two thirds of each House, remove such disability.

Section 4. The validity of the public debt of the United States, authorized by law, including debts incurred for payment of pensions and bounties for services in suppressing insurrection or rebellion, shall not be questioned. But neither the United States nor any State shall assume or pay any debt or obligation incurred in aid of insurrection or rebellion against the United States, or any claim for the loss or emancipation of any slave; but all such debts, obligations, and claims shall be held illegal and void.

Section 5. The Congress shall have power to enforce, by appropriate legislation, the provisions of this article.

AMENDMENT XV [Ratified March 30, 1870]
Section 1. The right of citizens of the United States to vote shall not be denied or abridged by the United States or by any State on account of race, color, or previous condition of servitude.
Section 2. The Congress shall have power to enforce this article by appropriate legislation.

AMENDMENT XVI [Ratified February 25, 1913]
The Congress shall have power to lay and collect taxes on incomes, from whatever source derived, without apportionment among the several States, and without regard to any census or enumeration.

AMENDMENT XVII [Ratified May 31, 1913]
The Senate of the United States shall be composed of two senators from each State, elected by the people thereof, for six years; and each senator shall have one vote. The electors in each State shall have the qualifications requisite for electors of the most numerous branch of the State legislature.

When vacancies happen in the representation of any State in the Senate, the executive authority of such State shall issue writs of election to fill such vacancies: *Provided,* That the legislature of any State may empower the executive thereof to make temporary appointments until the people fill the vacancies by election as the legislature may direct.

This amendment shall not be so construed as to affect the election or term of any senator chosen before it becomes valid as part of the Constitution.

AMENDMENT XVIII[10] [Ratified January 29, 1919]
After one year from the ratification of this article, the manufacture, sale, or transportation of intoxicating liquors within, the importation thereof into, or the exportation thereof from the United States and all territory subject to the jurisdiction thereof for beverage purposes is thereby prohibited.

The Congress and the several States shall have concurrent power to enforce this article by appropriate legislation.

This article shall be inoperative unless it shall have been ratified as an amendment to the Constitution by the legislatures of the several States, as provided in the Constitution, within seven years from the date of the submission hereof to the States by Congress.

AMENDMENT XIX [Ratified August 26, 1920]
The right of citizens of the United States to vote shall not be denied or abridged by the United States or by any State on account of sex.

Congress shall have the power to enforce this article by appropriate legislation.

AMENDMENT XX [Ratified January 23, 1933]
Section 1. The terms of the President and Vice President shall end at noon on the 20th day of January, and the

[10] Repealed by the 21st Amendment.

terms of Senators and Representatives at noon on the 3d day of January, of the years in which such terms would have ended if this article had not been ratified; and the terms of their successors shall then begin.
Section 2. The Congress shall assemble at least once in every year, and such meeting shall begin at noon on the 3d day of January, unless they shall by law appoint a different day.
Section 3. If, at the time fixed for the beginning of the term of President, the President-elect shall have died, the Vice President-elect shall become President. If a President shall not have been chosen before the time fixed for the beginning of his term, or if the President-elect shall have failed to qualify, then the Vice President-elect shall act as President until a President shall have qualified; and the Congress may by law provide for the case wherein neither a President-elect nor a Vice President-elect shall have qualified, declaring who shall then act as President, or the manner in which one who is to act shall be selected, and such person shall act accordingly until a President or Vice President shall have qualified.
Section 4. The Congress may by law provide for the case of the death of any of the persons from whom the House of Representatives may choose a President whenever the right of choice shall have devolved upon them, and for the case of the death of any of the persons from whom the Senate may choose a Vice President whenever the right of choice shall have devolved upon them.
Section 5. Sections 1 and 2 shall take effect on the 15th day of October following the ratification of this article.
Section 6. This article shall be inoperative unless it shall have been ratified as an amendment to the Constitution by the legislatures of three-fourths of the several States within seven years from the date of its submission.

AMENDMENT XXI [Ratified December 5, 1933]
Section 1. The Eighteenth Article of amendment to the Constitution of the United States is hereby repealed.
Section 2. The transportation or importation into any State, Territory, or possession of the United States for delivery or use therein of intoxicating liquors in violation of the laws thereof, is hereby prohibited.
Section 3. This article shall be inoperative unless it shall have been ratified as an amendment to the Constitution by conventions in the several States as provided in the Constitution, within seven years from the date of the submission thereof to the States by the Congress.

AMENDMENT XXII [Ratified March 1, 1951]
No person shall be elected to the office of the President more than twice, and no person who has held the office of President, or acted as President, for more than two years of a term to which some other person was elected President shall be elected to the office of the President more than once.

But this article shall not apply to any person holding the office of President when this article was proposed by the Congress, and shall not prevent any person who may be holding the office of President, or acting as President, during the term within which this article becomes operative from holding the office of President or acting as President during the remainder of such term.

This article shall be inoperative unless it shall have been ratified as an amendment to the Constitution by the legislatures of three-fourths of the several States within seven years from the date of its submission to the States by the Congress.

AMENDMENT XXIII [Ratified March 29, 1961]

Section 1. The District constituting the seat of Government of the United States shall appoint in such manner as the Congress may direct:

A number of electors of President and Vice President equal to the whole number of Senators and Representatives in Congress to which the District would be entitled if it were a State, but in no event more than the least populous State; they shall be in addition to those appointed by the States, but they shall be considered, for the purposes of the election of President and Vice President, to be electors appointed by a State; and they shall meet in the District and perform such duties as provided by the twelfth article of amendment.

Section 2. The Congress shall have power to enforce this article by appropriate legislation.

AMENDMENT XXIV [Ratified January 23, 1964]

Section 1. The right of citizens of the United States to vote in any primary or other election for President or Vice President, for electors for President or Vice President, or for Senator or Representative in Congress, shall not be denied or abridged by the United States or any State by reason of failure to pay any poll tax or other tax.

Section 2. The Congress shall have power to enforce this article by appropriate legislation.

AMENDMENT XXV [Ratified February 10, 1967]

Section 1. In case of the removal of the President from office or of his death or resignation, the Vice President shall become President.

Section 2. Whenever there is a vacancy in the office of the Vice President, the President shall nominate a Vice President who shall take office upon confirmation by a majority vote of both Houses of Congress.

Section 3. Whenever the President transmits to the President pro tempore of the Senate and the Speaker of the House of Representatives his written declaration that he is unable to discharge the powers and duties of his office, and until he transmits to them a written declaration to the contrary, such powers and duties shall be discharged by the Vice President as Acting President.

Section 4. Whenever the Vice President and a majority of either the principal officers of the executive departments or of such other body as Congress may by law provide, transmit to the President pro tempore of the Senate and the Speaker of the House of Representatives their written declaration that the President is unable to discharge the powers and duties of his office, the Vice President shall immediately assume the powers and duties of the office as Acting President.

Thereafter, when the President transmits to the President pro tempore of the Senate and the Speaker of the House of Representatives his written declaration that no inability exists, he shall resume the powers and duties of his office unless the Vice President and a majority of either the principal officers of the executive departments or of such other body as Congress may by law provide, transmit within four days to the President pro tempore of the Senate and the Speaker of the House of Representatives their written declaration that the President is unable to discharge the powers and duties of his office. Thereupon Congress shall decide the issue, assembling within forty-eight hours for that purpose if not in session. If the Congress, within twenty-one days after receipt of the latter written declaration, or, if Congress is not in session, within twenty-one days after Congress is required to assemble, determines by two-thirds vote of both Houses that the President is unable to discharge the powers and duties of his office, the Vice President shall continue to discharge the same as Acting President; otherwise, the President shall resume the powers and duties of his office.

Index

273